SOUTH DEVON COLLEGE LIBRARY

Tackling child poverty in the UK

An end in sight?

Edited by Geoff Fimister

CPAG • 94 White Lion Street • London N1 9PF

CPAG promotes action for the relief, directly or indirectly, of poverty among children and families with children. We work to ensure that those on low incomes get their full entitlements to welfare benefits. In our campaigning and information work we seek to improve benefits and policies for low-income families in order to eradicate the injustice of poverty. If you are not already supporting us, please consider making a donation, or ask for details of our membership schemes and publications.

Poverty Publication 102

Published by CPAG
94 White Lion Street, London N1 9PF

© CPAG 2001

ISBN 1 901698 34 3

The views expressed in this book are the authors' and do not necessarily express those of CPAG.

A CIP record for this book is available from the British Library

Cover and design by Devious Designs 0114 275 5634
Typeset by Boldface 020 7253 2014
Printed by Russell Press 0115 978 4505

CONTENTS

ACKNOWLEDGEMENTS

I would like to thank all the authors for so generously giving up their time to contribute to this publication. Thanks are also due to Ruth Lister and Carol Walker for their invaluable comments on the early drafts, and to Gill Scott and Usha Brown for commenting on the draft chapters in the context of Scotland.

Jonathan Bradshaw is grateful for the help of Holly Sutherland, David Piachaud and Paul Nicholson. Martin Barnes and I would also like to thank Fiona Frobisher, Peter Golding, Beth Lakhani, Ruth Lister and John Veit-Wilson for their very helpful comments on an earlier version of Chapter 2.

Thanks are also due to Alison Key for managing the production of the book and to Paula McDiarmid for proofreading the text.

Geoff Fimister

ABOUT THE CONTRIBUTORS

Pete Alcock is Professor of Social Policy and Administration and Head of the Department of Social Policy and Social Work at the University of Birmingham. He is the author of *Understanding Poverty and Social Policy in Britain*, as well as a number of other books and articles on poverty, social security and social policy.

Martin Barnes is Director of the Child Poverty Action Group.

Jonathan Bradshaw is Professor of Social Policy at the University of York and Associate Director of the Social Policy Research Unit. He is President of the Federation for International Studies in Social Security (FISS) and Chair of York Welfare Benefits Unit.

Gary Craig is Professor of Social Justice at the University of Hull. Prior to working within academic settings he worked in local government and the voluntary sector in a range of community development projects. His research interests include race and ethnicity, community development, local governance, and poverty and social inclusion.

George Davey Smith is Professor of Clinical Epidemiology in the Department of Social Medicine, University of Bristol. His research interests relate to how influences over the lifecourse affect adult disease risks.

Daniel Dorling is Professor of Quantitative Human Geography at the University of Leeds. His current research interests include mapping and measuring the changing distribution of poverty in Britain and measures to alleviate it.

Richard Exell is the TUC's Senior Policy Officer responsible for Welfare to Work issues. He is a member of the Disability Rights Commission and the Social Security Advisory Committee.

Geoff Fimister is part-time Research Officer at the Child Poverty

Action Group and a freelance writer and consultant on benefit policy issues.

David Gordon is Senior Research Fellow in the School for Policy Studies at the University of Bristol. His research interests include housing policy, crime, the scientific measurement of poverty and the causal effects of poverty on ill health.

Ruth Lister is Professor of Social Policy at Loughborough University.

Tim Marsh is Policy Officer for the UK Public Health Association and formerly Information Officer at CPAG.

Mary Shaw is an ESRC Research Fellow in the School of Geographical Sciences at the University of Bristol. Her research interests include social and spatial health inequalities in Britain.

George Smith is a researcher in the Department of Social Policy and Social Work at the University of Oxford. He has been involved with education and disadvantage for many years and currently specialises in the measurement of these at a local level.

Teresa Smith is a researcher in the Department of Social Policy and Social Work at the University of Oxford, specialising in pre-school educational provision and disadvantage.

Matthew Waters works in Shelter's Policy Unit. He has specific responsibility for benefits policy and its impact on homelessness and housing need.

FOREWORD

An End in Sight? Tackling child poverty in the UK is the latest in a long line of pre-election analyses published by CPAG in order to scrutinise the Government's record and to attempt to make poverty an election issue. Poverty was not an issue at the last election, reflecting the growing political as well as social and economic exclusion of those in poverty. Nevertheless, within a few months of taking office, the Prime Minister wrote that 'Yes, we are the party of Middle Britain, but if we don't raise the standard of living of the poorest people in Britain we will have failed as a government.'[1]

The early signals were that we could not expect anything so 'old Labour' as redistribution and improvements to out-of-work benefit levels to achieve this aspiration, despite the massive increase in inequality over the previous two decades. Such an approach was associated with a *status quo*, which promoted passive 'welfare dependency', in contrast to empowerment through paid work. Yet the cumulative impact of Labour budgets has been progressive, 'with significant gains at the bottom and small losses at the top'.[2] And an important element has been significant improvements in the real value of income support rates for younger children.

Looking over its shoulder at Middle Britain, the Government has kept remarkably quiet about some of these measures, covering its tracks with the use of 'tough' language, such as 'the end of a something-for-nothing welfare state'. In many ways this is astute politics. It is, though, problematic, for at least three reasons:

1. The tough language constructs social security recipients as 'other' to 'us' the taxpayers. By creating a negative image of the 'welfare dependant', it sends out messages, which could undermine the Prime Minister's call, in his 1999 Beveridge Lecture, for us to recapture the earlier popularity of the welfare state. At the same time the onwards drift down the road of means-testing runs the risk of separating benefit recipients further from the rest of society.
2. 'To do good by stealth' may not be reaping the hoped-for political rewards in 'the Labour heartlands'.[3] If this is the case, the lesson is

not to back-pedal on the policy, but to pursue it with more conviction and with an unambiguous message to the country as a whole.

3. This message has to include making the case for progressive taxation as an instrument of social justice and an expression of citizenship responsibility.[4]

In his recent 'green' speech, Tony Blair spoke of the conflict faced by politicians who need both to 'woo' and to 'lead' the electorate. The time has come for the Government to show the same unequivocal leadership in the crusade against domestic poverty as it is providing in the global arena in relation to poverty in developing countries. Its approach to international development, which emphasises participation in decision-making processes as a human right, also has implications for the domestic politics of poverty.[5] Likewise, principles of global social justice and social inclusion should be applied to the treatment of asylum seekers.

The desire of politicians to woo 'Middle Britain' must not result once again in the marginalisation of poverty as an election issue. I hope that this book will be used to put poverty and inequality on the agenda by all those committed to a more just and equal society.

Ruth Lister

1   *Independent*, 8 December 1997
2   J Hills, *Taxation for the Enabling State*, CASE, 2000
3   See Martin Barnes' editorial in *Poverty* 106, CPAG
4   See the report of the Commission on Taxation and Citizenship, *Paying for Progress*, Fabian Society, 2000
5   See Department for International Development, *Human Rights for Poor People*, February 2000; and *Listen Hear. the right to be heard*, Report of the Commission on Poverty, Participation and Power, Policy Press, 2000

Introduction

Geoff Fimister

On 4 October 2000 I found myself in a hotel in Bournemouth speaking on the same platform as Conservative social security spokesperson, David Willetts MP, and Lorna Reith of the Disability Alliance, on the subject of ending child poverty. The occasion was a fringe meeting at the Conservative Party Conference. Naturally, the views of the contributors did not necessarily coincide, but a lively and constructive discussion ensued and indeed continued long after the formal close of the meeting.

Two points struck me in particular about this debate. Firstly, while there was plenty of discussion and disagreement about how poverty might be defined, nobody seemed to be suggesting that it was synonymous with outright destitution: the notion of a social context appeared to be accepted. Given that the previous government took the view that poverty was a very bad thing – so it was jolly fortunate that there was none in the UK – this was welcome. It may be that the audience was simply humouring the 'outside' speakers, but I prefer to think that the recent high profile of the poverty debate has indeed raised the level of sophistication with which the subject is approached.

Secondly, I was interested in the view of one Conservative local councillor who expressed surprise at CPAG's willingness to engage with all of the main political parties: he had assumed that we would simply fall in behind a Labour government. Clearly, he knew little of CPAG's colourful history in this respect. In 1968, Richard Crossman, irritated by what he saw as the overly critical attitude of certain Labour Party officials towards, amongst other things, Labour's record on poverty, was moved to complain that 'it was a document which the

CPAG could have published, and that's saying a lot'.[1] This presaged the *contretemps* between CPAG and the Wilson Government in 1970 over that very issue,[2] referred to by Jonathan Bradshaw in the opening lines of his contribution to this book. Then there was Frank Field's run-in, when he was CPAG's Director, with the Callaghan regime over the threatened postponement of the introduction of child benefit – a clash which involved leaked Cabinet minutes and enormous controversy.[3]

Certainly, the continuous erosion of benefit entitlements during the long years of the Thatcher and Major governments was bound to entail a severe clash of perspectives with groups such as CPAG. Nevertheless, the plain fact is that our role is to campaign against poverty, whoever is in office – and the record bears this out.

So how does this square with our experience of the Labour government since 1997?

A CHANGE OF GOVERNMENT

The process of lobbying around benefits legislation over a number of years meant that the 'poverty lobby' had frequently found itself briefing the then Opposition and discussing with it what an anti-poverty strategy ought to look like. But opposition is one thing and government another. CPAG was not naïve enough to expect, in 1997, the advent of an era of calm seas and plain sailing. Nor were we cynical enough to expect nothing to be different. We considered that our role was to press on with our arguments, to give credit where credit was due and to criticise as and when necessary.

It was clear at the outset[4] that we would not see the sort of redistributive strategy for which the poverty lobby has traditionally argued. Nor did we expect the reversal of such much-decried Conservative measures as the weakening of state pensions; the abolition of single payments and their replacement by the social fund; or the cuts associated with the introduction of incapacity benefit and the jobseeker's allowance.

On the other hand, the new government clearly saw the benefit system as a major target for reform. The Welfare to Work programme, with its New Deals for various groups, was the main vehicle intended to bring about the changes which the Government wished to see. This programme had many positive aspects, but it seemed unbalanced – as if low-paid work, shored up by a minimum wage and in-work benefits, would provide most of the answers to the long-standing problems of the benefit system. Major reviews and proposals for change were set in motion in a number of areas of the system, together with several smaller- scale initiatives – but all against a background which seemed to see benefits for non-workers merely as a burden.

From an anti-poverty perspective, there was indeed both good and bad news. The measures which emerged could be divided into three groups:

- 'Pipeline' changes, which the previous government had already announced and incorporated into spending plans. These were largely carried through unchanged by the new regime. Cuts to lone parents' benefits proved especially controversial – an issue which Jonathan Bradshaw identifies as one of the Government's low points in terms of addressing poverty.
- Further options for change which the previous government had under consideration. These were fed, as possibilities, into the new government's various reviews and in a number of cases were leaked. Options (some of which indeed came to pass) for cuts to disability benefits again aroused heated controversy.
- The new government's long-term proposals. It is these which the various reviews were intended to formulate and something of which emerged in the March 1998 Budget and subsequent social security Green Paper.[5]

The Green Paper set out eight 'key principles' which would 'guide our reform programme'.[6] It is worth setting these out in full:

- The new welfare state should help and encourage people of working age to work where they are capable of doing so.
- The public and private sectors should work in partnership to ensure that, wherever possible, people are insured against foreseeable risks and make provision for their retirement.
- The new welfare state should provide public services of high quality to the whole community, as well as cash benefits.
- Those who are disabled should get the support they need to lead a fulfilling life with dignity.
- The system should support families and children, as well as tackling the scourge of child poverty.
- There should be specific action to attack social exclusion and help those in poverty.
- The system should encourage openness and honesty and the gateways to benefit should be clear and enforceable.

- The system of delivering modern welfare should be flexible, efficient and easy for people to use.

These principles are for the most part uncontroversial, but were sufficiently broad to accommodate a wide range of potential specific measures. Moreover, their generally positive tone contrasted uncomfortably with the cuts to lone parents' benefits and the controversy over disability benefits. It seemed that very mixed messages were being given to the general public and to the Labour Party faithful. As a specialist in benefit policy, I received during this period many requests to speak at meetings – including at a number of Labour Party branches – where the general drift of questioning from the audience was 'what on earth is going on?'

Another part of the puzzle was the announcement, in August 1997, of the establishment of the Social Exclusion Unit (SEU) – the work of which is referred to by several of our contributors. This was to be a Cabinet Office unit with a remit to identify and promote measures to tackle 'social exclusion'. But it seemed that there were potential policy contradictions here. On the one hand, the Welfare to Work programme, if it succeeded in achieving a lasting increase in the number of people in work, could make a real contribution to efforts to combat social exclusion. On the other, some of the benefit cuts which had been announced or were under consideration seemed to have much greater potential for increasing social exclusion than the SEU had to reduce it. Anti-poverty campaigners warned that the objectives of the SEU needed to inform the benefit reviews if such contradictions were to be avoided.

In the event, things began to change for the better. At first, the development of the working families' tax credit as the flagship benefit measure, aimed very much at 'making work pay', seemed to be leaving behind the problems of those for whom work was not an option. But the Budget of March 1998 marked the beginning of a process which has injected significant resources into the incomes of families with children, whether or not the parents are in work. And of course in March 1999 came the Prime Minister's announcement of the intention to abolish child poverty in 20 years. Whatever one might say about the definition of poverty, the rate of change and the clarity of the indicators of progress – all of which considerations are aired in this book – there is no doubt that this was an historic commitment, warmly welcomed by CPAG. No, we did not feel that the Government had 'shot our fox' (to use a topical metaphor). Rather, we recognised that here was an opportunity to achieve a much higher profile for the poverty debate and to secure some very real gains for families on low incomes.

Making sure that this impetus is maintained is, of course, a major challenge for both the Government and the poverty lobby – especially if changes of political administration or in economic circumstances (see below) intervene. Doubtless, also, there will be many disagreements over specific measures. Nevertheless, the agenda has changed in a very real way.

So how do we explain these changes of direction, shifts of emphasis and mixed messages since 1997? The following can all be advanced as possibilities:

- The Government was jolted by the reaction, especially from within the Labour Party, to the cuts in lone parents' and some disability benefits.
- The Welfare to Work programme is key to the Government's approach and is very much designed to make use of both carrots and sticks.
- Politically, the Government tries to keep on board a wide range of opinion and tends to seek to balance progressive social measures with tabloid-friendly rhetoric.
- The improved state of the public finances, whatever its cause, has created much greater latitude for anti-poverty measures.

No doubt all of these factors play some part in explaining both changes in policies over the last few years and in the general tenor of government statements at different times and in different contexts. There is no doubt, though, that a key part of the explanation for the shift in policy is the pre-election commitment by the Labour Party to remain within the previous government's spending plans for two years; and not to increase income tax rates during the course of the Parliament. This severely restricted initial spending options. Some felt that New Labour's original Secretary of State for Social Security could have fought her corner harder and not delivered the required cuts so easily. This may or may not be true. But there is no doubt that the subsequent easing of the financial straitjacket changed the rules of the game – which should, of course, make us worry as to how well the current concern with poverty would weather a tougher economic climate.

POVERTY – THE ISSUES

When CPAG began planning this 'pre-election' book, we took as our starting point the need for a relatively short publication which could be read reasonably easily by busy politicians, commentators and voters, but which would be lengthy enough to provide some useful information and analysis. We decided on two longer chapters, the first of which – by Jonathan Bradshaw – would examine the Government's record in pursuit of its pledge to abolish child poverty and would offer some observations on the scale and nature of the remaining task. In doing this, Bradshaw has some very interesting things to say about the change of focus, after the first two years, to which I refer above.

Martin Barnes and I wrote the second of our longer chapters, intended to home in on the current debate concerning the future of children's benefits. The integrated child credit could amount to a real step forward, or it could be full of pitfalls. These issues need to be debated and not mentally filed away as a complex matter best left to technical specialists. At a time when an impending general election coincides with the planning stages of this major new initiative, this is especially important.

Our aim was then to invite a number of authors from various fields to examine, in half a dozen shorter chapters, some of the other dimensions of poverty; to tell us how they rated the Government's performance so far; and to map out the tasks which the next administration would need to address if the commitment to combat poverty is to be carried forward. Thus, Richard Exell looks at employment policy – an area upon which, as noted above, the Government places great reliance for the success of its overall anti-poverty strategy; George Smith looks at education – another of the Government's key policy areas, not least in its interaction with employment prospects; Mary Shaw and her colleagues examine the relationship between health and poverty – a link which, it now seems strange to recall, governments not so long ago used to deny; Matthew Waters tackles housing – its supply and affordability, including the vexed question of housing benefit; Pete Alcock delves into the complex interrelationships which surround the question of neighbourhood renewal; and Gary Craig addresses the racial dimension and the degree to which the Government has devised an adequate policy response.

Clearly, there are other aspects and manifestations of poverty which we could have addressed, but given the scale and purpose of the book, we had to make choices. It is very likely that many readers would have made different choices, arguably just as valid. For example, we could have devoted a chapter to an overall analysis of the way the benefit system has developed under New Labour, in terms both of its structure (the continuing decline of contributory benefits, more reliance on means-testing, the emergence of tax credits) and its administration (the creation of the new agency structure, the growing prominence of anti-fraud measures, the new role of the Inland Revenue). Or we could have grouped together the issues affecting women, who constitute the majority of benefit claimants, the great majority of lone parents and who usually have the main caring role in two-parent households with dependent children – but who frequently face disadvantage when resources are allocated, whether within the family or through the wage structure. Or we could have devoted a chapter to the particular problems of disabled people, both within the out-of-work benefit system and in employment. Or we could have looked harder at the devolution agenda: social security is a function reserved to the UK government, but this has not prevented the devolved administrations from taking a particular interest in poverty. Scotland is perhaps especially noteworthy, with its explicit recognition of the importance of *inequality* and its linking of social exclusion to the concept of social *justice*. Then there is the question of how people living in poverty can themselves organise and have a voice in the fight against it.[7] And there is the international dimension, by which I do not simply mean European issues or comparisons with the United States: as pressure on the planet's resources grow, poverty will increasingly have to be addressed in a global context – we are, in a very real sense, all in this together.

These are all themes to which CPAG will undoubtedly return – but for now, we offer this book as a contribution to the pre-election debate here in the UK. The material it contains was written towards the end of 2000 and such is the current rate of change that there will doubtless have been further developments in some areas by the time of the general election campaign. But the key issues are clear enough. The fate of the Government's current anti-poverty initiatives will tell us much about the political values which this country will take forward into the twenty-first century.

NOTES

1 R Crossman, *The Diaries of a Cabinet Minister: Vol 2, Lord President of the Council and Leader of the House of Commons 1966-68*, Hamish Hamilton and Jonathan Cape, 1976, p656

2 Child Poverty Action Group, *Poverty and the Labour Government*, CPAG, 1970

3 F Field, 'Killing a Commitment: the Cabinet v the Children', *New Society*, 17 June 1976; see also E Jacobs and P Kellner, 'Purse or Wallet? How the Cabinet did a switch-sell', *Sunday Times*, 20 June 1976

4 This account updates an analysis which the author originally published in *The Benefits Agenda: an analysis of the Government's reviews and proposals*, Newcastle Welfare Rights Service, Newcastle upon Tyne City Council, 1997 and 1998

5 Department of Social Security, *New Ambitions for Our Country: a new contract for welfare*, Cm 3805, The Stationery Office, March 1998

6 See note 5, p2

7 For a recent example of CPAG's interest in this area, see P Beresford, D Green, R Lister and K Woodard, *Poverty First Hand: poor people speak for themselves*, CPAG, 1999

Child poverty under Labour
Jonathan Bradshaw

INTRODUCTION

In the weeks leading up to the general election in 1970 the Child Poverty Action Group published a pamphlet (written by Frank Field and Peter Townsend) maintaining that poor people had become worse off under Labour. The Tories under Ted Heath won the election, to the surprise of many pundits.

CPAG would not be justified if it were to assert the same at the next election. There is no doubt that when the election takes place there will have been a substantial reduction in poverty, particularly child poverty, by any measure you care to use. This is a great achievement. It reverses a trend of dramatically increasing child poverty rates during the 1980s and no diminution during the 1990s. This reduction in child poverty has been achieved, of course, partly as a consequence of a buoyant economy with falling unemployment. But mainly it has been the result of pursuing redistributive social and fiscal policies, and it has been this factor that contrasts the Labour achievements most starkly with the Tory governments after 1979.

But although child poverty will have fallen by the time of the election, the fall could have started earlier and proceeded faster. Given the economic, political and demographic conditions since the 1997 election, those who support CPAG have every reason to be disappointed. Redistributive social policies have not been used well enough, early enough. In fact, the first two years of this Government's term in office were dire for poor children. As a result, as we shall see, because of the time it takes to analyse the *Family Resources Survey* and publish *Households Below Average Income* (HBAI), the Government will probably enter the next election with the 1998/99 HBAI showing no evidence that by then they had actually reduced child poverty.

The Prime Minister's historic commitment (two years *after* the election) in March 1999 to end child poverty in 20 years was both welcome and brave – and unexpected in the light of the Government's first two years. But the commitment is also far too leisurely – not now, not in ten years, but after 20 years. Meanwhile, another generation of children are to be condemned to be raised in poverty. This timescale might have been justified for a government short of resources or appropriate political support, but it is totally unacceptable for a government with so much resources that it has been able to cut the standard rate of income tax (implemented in 2000/01).

In this chapter I shall review the Government's achievements in more detail. But first, let us establish the child poverty situation when Labour came to power in 1997.

CHILD POVERTY IN 1997

Figure 1 shows that by 1996/97 the proportion of children living in households below 50 per cent of the contemporary average income after housing costs had increased to 35 per cent. This was an increase from 10 per cent in 1979. Most of this increase occurred during the early Thatcher years and during the Lawson boom in the late 1980s. During the 1990s there had been little change in the (very high) rates of child poverty. By 1998/99 (the latest data available) there was no evidence of a reduction since Labour came to power.[1]

Many will be critical of this measure of poverty. However, there are three other sources of evidence that confirm this picture.

• Using a poverty threshold that does not move with average income shows that the number of children living in real 1979 terms poverty increased by 300,000 between 1979 and 1995/96[2] – a period when average incomes increased in real terms by over 40 per cent.
• Figure 2 shows that the proportion of children living in families dependent on income support increased from less than 5 per cent in 1979, peaked at 25.7 per cent in 1993 and had fallen only to 18.4 per cent by May 2000. This is over a period when social assistance rates were more or less frozen in real terms.
• Two surveys were undertaken in 1983 and 1990 using *Breadline*

Britain methods.[3] The proportion of households lacking three or more socially perceived necessities increased from 14 per cent in 1983 to 21 per cent in 1990 and to 24 per cent in 1999.[4]

These formal measures of poverty are supported by evidence of a deterioration in the well-being of children. The increase in child poverty has been associated with increased inequality in respect of child mortality, low birth weight, child accidents, teenage pregnancy, bad housing conditions, educational attainment and suicide – in respect of each of these the gap between poor children and the rest has been increasing. Other outcomes associated with child poverty have not improved as much as they might have.[5]

Perhaps as startling as this national evidence of child poverty is the international evidence,[6] using a variety of different sources of data, which confirms that Britain had the highest child poverty rates in the mid 1990s of any country in the European Union and one of the highest in the industrial world – only exceeded by Russia and the USA. Further, they show that child poverty in the UK increased more than almost any other country between the early 1980s and the mid 1990s. This suggests that increasing child poverty was not the result of great movements such as demographic transitions or globalisation. Or rather, during this period many countries managed to use social policies to protect and even improve the living standards of families with children. The comparative evidence also demonstrates that the UK has a high child poverty rate pre-transfer (before the impact of taxes and benefits) – as a result of the market forces – high rates of workless households containing children, low lone parent labour supply and low earnings. But we were not out of line with some other countries in these respects. What is really responsible for our high child poverty rates is the comparative inadequacy of our social protection system – both the child benefit package for those parents with low earnings, and the out-of-work package for those families with children dependent on the social security benefits. Children are more likely to be poor in the UK than in other countries because of the failure of policy makers to protect them – to protect children as well as other countries do.

This is the legacy of the Tory years and it should not be forgotten. There is no indication that the Tories have acknowledged the damage that their policies caused for children, nor that in a future term of office they will behave differently. This should be taken into account in what comes next.

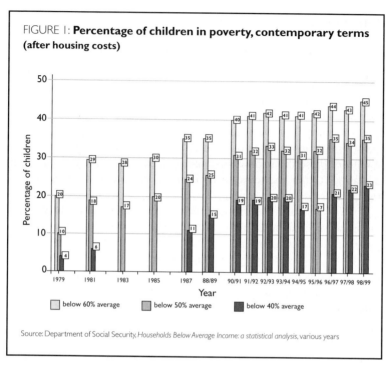

FIGURE 1: **Percentage of children in poverty, contemporary terms (after housing costs)**

Source: Department of Social Security, *Households Below Average Income: a statistical analysis*, various years

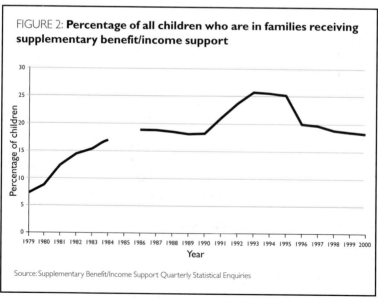

FIGURE 2: **Percentage of all children who are in families receiving supplementary benefit/income support**

Source: Supplementary Benefit/Income Support Quarterly Statistical Enquiries

CHILD POVERTY AFTER 1997

In 1997, after 17 years of Conservative rule, a Labour government came to power. Before the election Tony Blair had declared 'If the next Labour government has not raised the living standards of the poorest by the end of its time in office it will have failed.'[7] But prior to the election the Labour leadership made the (totally unnecessary) pledges to stick to Tory spending plans for two years and not to increase direct taxation during this Parliament. Given the parliamentary majority they achieved and the public will to see change associated with it, we can claim (admittedly with hindsight) that these pledges were ill-advised. But what appalled Labour supporters was the zeal with which the leadership and the new MPs stuck to these commitments, despite the fact that their first victims were poor children living in lone-parent families.

Almost the Labour Government's first social policy act was to implement a Tory plan to abolish the lone parent premium in income support and one parent benefit. The consequence was that about two million of the poorest children in Britain would have been worse off (eventually – existing claimants did not lose the benefits – for them they would wither away, but new or repeat claimants would not be eligible). The cut in income support for lone parents was arguably[8] the first real terms cut in the level of social assistance paid to any group of claimants since social assistance was introduced in 1948 – a grave precedent. The abolition of one parent benefit was in direct conflict with Labour's espoused policy to encourage lone parents into the labour market (this benefit increased out-of-work income, but was fully taken into account in income support). No doubt partly as a result, the 1998/99 *Households Below Average Income* figures (see Figure 1) show an increase in child poverty over 1997/98. This is the record that the Labour Government will have when it goes to the country – more or less entirely the consequence of its own policies.

This is not the place to dwell on why this terrible social policy measure was implemented. However, it is regrettable to record that it was proposed by a Secretary of State who had been the legal officer of the National Council for Civil Liberties, with the support of a Minister of State who had been Director of the Child Poverty Action Group, and with enthusiastic supporting speeches during the Second Reading from the former Director of the Low Pay Unit as well as many other Labour MPs who have been members of CPAG. It is now generally acknowledged as the most bruising experience of this Labour

Government, resulting from a huge outcry inside and outside Parliament. It also lost the Government the support of almost the whole of the informed social policy constituency.

A very bad start, but this experience may have contributed to the shift in policy that has resulted in child poverty now being at the centre of Labour's domestic policy. Anyway, the state of child poverty in the UK and the evidence of our comparative position had begun to seep into the political consciousness. On 18 March 1999 Tony Blair announced:

> Our historic aim will be for ours to be the first generation to end child poverty, and it will take a generation. It is a 20-year mission but I believe it can be done.

The policy chronology presented by Tim Marsh in the Appendix reveals the huge number of policy announcements that have now been made and which have a bearing on the child poverty commitment. The strategy can broadly be described under four headings:

- **Preventive measures**: including investment in education, the National Health Service, measures to reduce teenage pregnancies, the Sure Start programme, educational maintenance allowances and the Children's Fund.
- **Labour market measures** ('work for those who can'): including the minimum wage, economic management to maximise employment, the New Deals (particularly in this context the New Deal for lone parents), the Childcare Strategy, real increases in child benefit, working families' tax credit, childcare tax credit and child credits.
- **Social protection measures** ('security for those who can't'): including real increases in income support and changes to earnings disregards.
- **Neighbourhood measures**: New Deal for communities, Single Regeneration Budget, education action zones etc.

It is impossible to evaluate the success or otherwise of the preventive measures so early in the project. First, though, it should be noted that the Government's new-found concern about child poverty did not extend to the children of asylum seekers (see Chapter 8). There is some evidence (see below and Chapter 4) that the education standards strategy is bearing dividends – on average – and improving most the performance of children in the most deprived areas. The neighbourhood measures are dealt with in Chapter 7. The analysis in the rest of this chapter will mainly deal with the evidence of the outcomes of the dual strategy of 'work for those who can and security for those who can't'.

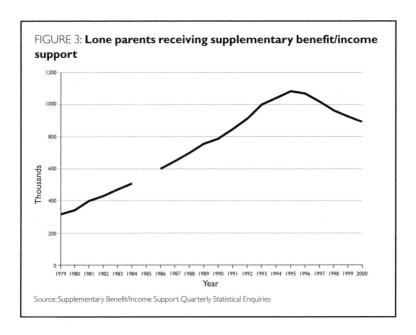

FIGURE 3: **Lone parents receiving supplementary benefit/income support**

Source: Supplementary Benefit/Income Support Quarterly Statistical Enquiries

LABOUR'S ACHIEVEMENTS

In evaluating government achievements in the field of child poverty, it is important to recognise that policy does not operate in a vacuum. In particular, it is very difficult to disentangle the impact of policy from the impact of economic and demographic factors, which are more or less independent from policy. Just to give a few examples:

• Demographic patterns will have an impact on child poverty rates. Thus, the increasing number of lone-parent families has been a factor driving up child poverty, as has their increased reliance on income support since the 1970s. Figure 3 shows trends in the number of lone parents receiving supplementary benefit/income support since 1979. But it is not just the number but also the characteristics of lone parents that influence child poverty rates. Single lone parents with young children are more likely to be poor than ex-married lone parents with older children – largely because the latter are more likely to be in employment. Also, as lone parents and their children grow older, they are more likely to be in employment. Although the rate of divorce has peaked, there appears to have been no diminution in relationship breakdown and the number of lone parents has continued to increase. However, it can be seen in Figure 3 that the number of lone parents dependent on income support has been falling from a peak of 1.056 million in 1995 to 910,000 in May 2000. Some of the recent decrease may be due to policies that may have influenced labour supply – the childcare disregard in family credit (a Tory measure), the minimum wage, the New Deal for lone parents, more generous in-work benefits including working families' tax credit and the childcare credit. But it is also a consequence of increased demand for labour associated with falling unemployment and the natural consequences of an ageing lone parent population.

• Unemployment was falling before Labour came to power and has continued to fall. The relationship between child poverty and official unemployment is not as close as many people might imagine. Lone-parent families, who in 1998/99 included 42 per cent of the children in the bottom quintile of the income distribution,[9] are not required to register for work and thus are not included in the unemployment count. Further, as Atkinson has shown, the overall unemployment rate and the percentage of children in households without a full-time worker has been diverging over the last two decades.[10] Nevertheless, as unemployment falls one can generally expect there to be a reduction in child poverty, because earnings plus in-work benefits are more likely to lift family income over a poverty threshold than out-of-work incomes.

So it is very difficult to distinguish the impact of policy from other factors.

There are three types of data available to evaluate the Government's child poverty strategy.

1. **Survey evidence or evidence from administrative statistics**. The Government has itself identified 13 indicators of this type, which it is using to monitor the success of the child poverty strategy in its *Opportunity for All* annual reports.[11] The problem with this type of data is that it takes time to emerge. I shall draw on the latest annual report, published in September 2000, and some other sources below.

2. **Evidence from policy simulations**. The second approach is to employ the technique of policy simulation to simulate the policies on a representative sample of the population and observe what impact they have on poverty rates. The Treasury has been doing this using government models in order for ministers to be able to make

claims about the number of children who are, or will be, lifted out of poverty by the policy measures that have been announced. However, the Government has not published any details of the evidence for these claims. Piachaud and Sutherland have undertaken similar analysis using POLIMOD.[12] They produced results for policies announced up to January 2000 and Sutherland has updated that analysis to include the announcements made in the April 2000 Budget.[13]

3. **Policy evaluations.** Then there are the results of the exercises that have been launched to monitor and evaluate the impact of specific policy initiatives. Perhaps the most important of these, for our purposes, is the evaluation of the New Deal for lone parents, which is dealt with in Chapter 3.

OPPORTUNITY FOR ALL

The Government published the second annual report, *The Changing Welfare State: Opportunity for All, One Year On: making a difference* in September 2000.[14] Table 1 summarises the findings relating to children and young people from that report. There are 13 indicators relating to children (in fact there are more because there are more than one statistic for each indicator). Two of the indicators have not yet got data attached to them (indicators 3 and 11) and indicator 8 only has baseline data because it is derived from the English House Conditions Survey, which is carried out only every five years. In the light of criticisms[15] of the indicators chosen in the first *Opportunity for All* report,[16] the Department of Social Security (DSS) has made a number of changes in the second report. It has dropped some of the proposed Sure Start indicators, introduced new indicators 5 and 13, redefined indicators 6 and 7, developed a new composite indicator on housing standards (8) and it is working on a new indicator which will provide evidence of the extent to which the target to narrow the gap in infant and early childhood mortality and morbidity between socio-economic groups is achieved. It is also proposing to introduce an indicator of the extent to which the gap is narrowed between the employment rates in the most deprived local authority districts and the overall employment rate. All this is to be welcomed.[17]

Let us turn to the picture revealed by the indicators. It can be seen from Table 1 that generally they are moving in the right direction. Only one, the teenage conception rate, shows an increase over the base line.

All others show either a stable situation or an improvement. In the summary report[18] the Government highlighted the following (with my comment in italics):

- Tax and benefit reforms announced in the last four budgets will lift 1.2 million children out of poverty. (*We need more detail*)
- Couples on income support with two children aged under 11 will

---

TABLE 1: **Summary of the *Opportunity for All* indicators for children and young people**

1. % children living in workless households	17.9 (1997)	17.9 (1998)	17.3 (1999)	15.8 (2000)
2a. % children living in households with income below 60% of the contemporary median before housing costs	26 (1996/97)	25 (1997/98)	24 (1998/99)	
2a. % children living in households with income below 60% of the median after housing costs	34 (1996/97)	33 (1997/98)	33 (1998/99)	
2b. % children living in households with income below 60 % of the 1996/97 median held constant in real terms before housing costs	26 (1996/97)	24 (1997/98)	22 (1998/99)	
2b. % children living in households with income below 60% of the 1996/97 median held constant in real terms after housing costs	34 (1996/97)	32 (1997/98)	31 (1998/99)	
2c. % of children experiencing persistent low income – below 60 % median household income in at least three out of four years	19 (1991-94)	17 (1995-98)		

2c. % children experiencing persistent low income – below 70% median household income in at least three out of four years	28 (1991-94)	26 (1995-98)			
3. % of seven-year-old children in Sure Start areas achieving Key Stage 1 English and maths tests					
4. % of those aged 11 achieving level 4 or above in Key Stage 2 tests for literacy	57 (1996)	63 (1997)	65 (1998)	71 (1999)	75 (2000)
4. % of those aged 11 achieving level 4 or above in Key Stage 2 tests for numeracy	54 (1996)	62 (1997)	59 (1998)	69 (1999)	72 (2000)
5. % of 16-year-olds with at least one GCSE A*-G	92.2 (1996)	92.3 (1997)	93.4 (1998)	94.0 (1999)	
6. % of 19-year-olds with at least a level 2 qualification or equivalent	70 (1996)	72 (1997)	74 (1998)	75 (1999)	
7. % truancies and school exclusions	0.17 (1995/96)	0.17 (1996/97)	0.16 (1997/98)	0.14 (1998/99)	
8. % of children who live in a home which falls below the set standard of decency	23 (1996)				
9. Admission rates (per thousand) to hospital as a result of an unintentional injury resulting in a stay of longer than three days for children aged under 16	1.20 (1996/97)	1.12 (1997/98)	1.02 (1998/99)		
10. % of 16-18-year-olds in learning	76 (1996)	75 (1997)	75 (1998)	75 (1999)	

11. % of young people leaving care with one of more GCSE (grade A*-G) or a vocational qualification					
12. Under 18 conception rates per 1000 aged 15-17	45.9 (1996)	45.5 (1997)	46.5 (1998)		
12. % of teenage parents who are not in education, employment or training	85 (1996)	84 (1997)	72 (1998)	74 (1999)	69 (2000)
13. % re-registered on the child protection register	19 (1997/98)	15 (1998/99)			

Source: Department of Social Security, *Opportunity for All, One Year On: making a difference, 2000*, Annex to the Second Annual Report, 2000

be nearly £30 a week better off in real terms from October 2000 compared with 1997. (*If they claim it*)

- Families on working families' tax credit receive on average £30 a week more than that under family credit. (*If they claim it*)
- The proportion of children living in workless households has fallen from 17.9 per cent in Spring 1997 to 15.8 per cent in Spring 2000 and there are 300,000 fewer children living in families claiming out-of-work benefits. (*The figure of 300,000 is for dependants under 19. The number of children (under 16) reliant on income support fell from 2.3 million in May 1997 to 2.16 million in May 2000*)
- 59 Sure Start programmes are up and running, a further 70 were due to start in Autumn 2000 and a further 65 in Autumn 2001.
- The proportion achieving the expected numeracy standard at age 11 is up from 54 per cent in 1996 to 72 per cent in 2000 and the majority of the most improved local authorities were in the inner cities.

THE POLIMOD ANALYSIS

The problem with the previous analysis based on survey or administrative data, is that it is out of date. For example, the latest HBAI analysis takes us to 1998/99 and therefore does not include the results of any of the changes announced in the 1999 and 2000 Budgets, without doubt the most important of the four Labour Budgets. At the time of writing, the latest administrative data on the number of children dependent on income support is for May 2000.

For these reasons, the simulations in the POLIMOD analysis are extremely valuable in providing up-to-date, indeed future, estimates of the likely impact of the Government's policies. POLIMOD is a static tax-benefit model which simulates the effects of tax and benefit changes on household incomes. It uses representative household micro-data based on the Family Expenditure Survey to calculate taxes and benefits before and after policy changes. It takes into account the latest evidence on non-take-up, but does not estimate any behavioural effects that might result from policy changes, though their analysis explores the sensitivity to changes in the labour force participation of parents. Following an analysis by Piachaud in 1998, Piachaud and Sutherland used POLIMOD to estimate the impact of policies announced up to January 2000.[19] This included the impact of the working families' tax credit from October 1999, real increases in child benefit in the 1999 and 2000 Budgets, the child tax credit due to be introduced by April 2001 and improvements in income support scales for children under 11 in October 1999 and April 2000. The simulations also took account of other measures announced in the 1998 and 1999 Budgets, the introduction of the national minimum wage and the abolition of lone parents' benefits mentioned above. They start with the policy rules in March 1997 and update their values to April 1999 using the Retail Price Index. They then take account of all the policy changes whether or not they were operational by the end of 1999. They calculate that the extra revenue costs of all these changes was £5.54 billion.

The picture presented by that analysis of POLIMOD was altered for the better by the analysis that Sutherland undertook in order to take account of the announcements made in the April 2000 Budget.[20] Among the measures announced in that budget that affected families with children were increases in the amounts for children in working families' tax credit from June 2000, increases in income support and other related benefits from October 2000, increases in child benefit and children's tax credit from April 2001 and an increase from £15 to £20 in the earnings disregard in income support/jobseeker's allowance. The additional revenue cost of the 2000 Budget was £2 billion.

Sutherland found that, post-Budget 2000, 91 per cent of children are in households who gain from the reforms. However, some lose and, although most of these are in better-off households, others, amounting to 2.3 per cent of all children, lose also, even though in the bottom decile of the income distribution. Thus, 300,000 of the poorest children are worse off. They tend to be in families not on income support who lose mortgage interest, or in households in receipt of income support with children over 11 who lose one parent benefit and premiums.

They also model the effect of these policies on the numbers of children living in families in poverty. Under April 1997 policy, 26.3 per cent of children were living in families with equivalised[21] income less than 50 per cent of average (before housing costs). Introducing Labour's changes reduces this poverty rate to 17 per cent or 9.3 percentage points (1.23 million children). These are substantial reductions in poverty. They also calculate that reductions in the poverty gap amount to 31.7 per cent – three-quarters of which is explained by increases in child benefit and social assistance. The additional impact of the April 2000 Budget is quite significant. An additional 390,000 children are shifted above the poverty line on top of the 840,000 removed by the previously announced changes.

The proportion of children in poverty *after housing costs* using the 50 per cent of mean threshold was 35 per cent in 1998/99. It should be noted that the Treasury (2000) has begun to use an after-housing costs measure of income and takes 60 per cent of the median as the poverty line. Sixty per cent of the median gives child poverty rates very close to 50 per cent of the mean. Unfortunately, however, POLIMOD does not generate after-housing costs poverty estimates so the numbers given in this paper are all before-housing costs. If we had had after-housing costs, estimates of the reduction in the child poverty rates achieved by the Government's measures would be lower.

Then there is the impact of falling unemployment. Piachaud and Sutherland also model the potential contribution of increased parental employment. Assuming at least one parent enters employment for a minimum of 30 hours on the minimum wage (which would require the creation of another 1.42 million jobs), they estimate that this would reduce child poverty by a further 970,000, or a total of 2.2 million children would be lifted out of poverty. This is almost certainly far too ambitious a hope – between 1997 and 2000 the proportion of children living in workless families fell from 17.9 per cent to 15.8 per cent (by only 11 per cent). There has been a fall of only 300,000 in the number of families with dependent children claiming out-of-work benefits (between May 1997 and May 2000). As we shall see in Chapter 4 the New Deal for lone parents has not yet had a major impact on the labour participation rate of this group. A much more realistic aspiration is that by 2001/02 'work for those who can' will have resulted in an increase in employment of 500,000 parents. This would result in a fall in child poverty of 320,000 which together with the tax and benefit changes would result in a fall in child poverty of 1.55 million to about half the pre-Labour policies level.

The general conclusion from this is that the Government has made good progress in raising the in-work incomes of poor working parents ('the work for those who can' part of the slogan) and, as long as the jobs can be found, its work strategy will further reduce child poverty. However, the policies of 'security for those who can't' have been much less developed. Only about half of parents of poor children are able to be helped by employment. The other half are self-employed, students, sick or disabled, parents of young children or other carers and those already working with low earnings. Despite the welcome increase in the income support scales from October 2000, the living standards of families with children on income support remain a good deal below the poverty level.

As a further reflection on this, it is worth comparing the level of income support paid with the 'low cost but adequate' budget devised by the Family Budget Unit.[22] Table 2 shows what has happened to income support scales for a lone parent and a couple both with two children under 11 compared with inflation and compared to the 'low cost but adequate' budget. By October 2000 the lone-parent family would be receiving £20.59 per week more than they would have received if income support rates had been increased in line with inflation. The couple family has done rather better (thanks to the fact that they did not suffer the loss of the lone parent premium) – they are £24.79 per week better off in real terms. The gap between the 'low cost but adequate' budget and income support has fallen to £5.95 for the lone-parent family (with children of these ages) and to £11.17 per week for the couple family.

These comparisons only allow for movements in the Retail Price Index (RPI). Over this period, earnings have increased faster than the RPI – thus between May 1997 and July 2000 the RPI rose by 8.7 per cent, earnings rose by 15.5 per cent and income support rose by 21.2 per cent for the lone-parent family and 22.7 per cent for the couple family. So couple families on income support have seen real improvements and have more than kept pace with earnings, while lone parents have seen real improvements, but thanks to the abolition of the lone parent premium have lost out in comparison with earnings.

TABLE 2: **Value of the income support scales over time and comparison with the FBU low cost but adequate budget**

	Lone parent plus two children under 11			Couple plus two children under 11		
	Income support per week	FBU low cost but adequate budget per week*	Shortfall per week	Income support per week	FBU low cost but adequate budget per week*	Shortfall per week
January 1998	£98.70	£122.21	−£23.51	£121.75	£154.04	−£32.29
Uprated by RPI** January 1998 to September 2000	£108.46	£134.30	−	£133.79	£169.27	−
Actual October 2000	£128.35	−	−£5.95	£158.10	−	−£11.17

*This is the FBU 'low cost but adequate' budget for these families (boy 10, girl 4) not in paid work and it excludes alcohol expenditure. It does not include the value of free milk tokens and vitamins and free school meals.
** Index less housing costs.

CONCLUSION

By the end of this Parliament, Labour will have achieved a reduction in child poverty. The Government has begun to use the tax and benefit system to help poor children and when the policies announced up to and including the 2000 Budget have been implemented, over 1.2 million children (above a third of the total) will have been lifted out of poverty (below half the average). Possibly another 320,000 will have been lifted out of poverty as a result of their parents obtaining employment. So Labour may have halved child poverty in five years rather than ten, on the before-housing costs measure.

But still more could have been achieved. Holly Sutherland was asked to estimate, using POLIMOD, what the impact on child poverty would have been if the resources foregone in the 1p cut in the standard rate of income tax had been used to increase the scales of income support for families with children. In that tax cut, £2.44 billion was foregone by the Treasury, enough to fund an increase in the children's income support rates to £45.60 (from £30.95 in October 2000). Over and above the reduction in child poverty achieved by measures announced up to and including the 2000 Budget, this would have reduced child poverty by a further 5.9 percentage points or 695,000 children. According to POLIMOD, in April 1997 there were 3.1 million children living in families with income below half the average. As we have seen, POLIMOD estimates that policies announced up to the 2000 Budget would have reduced that by 1.23 million. Increased employment may have contributed another 320,000 reduction. If the revenue foregone in the tax rate cut had been spent on increasing income support it would have fallen by a further 695,000. So if the resources foregone in the 1p cut had been used to increase the child scale rates in income support, along with the other changes, child poverty would have been reduced by 72 per cent on the before-housing costs basis.

Nevertheless, existing policies, would, if our labour supply estimates are correct, halve child poverty in five years not the ten years proposed. But that would still leave child poverty above the level it was when Labour left office in 1979 and still substantially higher than most other industrialised countries. Further, if Labour is really intent on this course then it has to focus on two issues.

First, the task is going to get harder – it has been relatively painless in terms of revenue (and taxation) to shift large numbers of poor children a little below the threshold to a little above it. But to lift those a long way below the threshold and every child some way above it will require more substantial investments, in particular in the level of income support for those who do not have access to the labour market.

Second, the child poverty reductions that we have observed have been generated by 'work for those who can' strategies and modest real improvements in child benefit and income support – relatively cheap financially and politically in terms of taxation and public expenditure. To achieve the objective of abolishing child poverty will eventually entail policies which are much tougher politically and much more redistributive. In order to abolish child poverty, income support is going to need to rise faster than the rate of inflation, faster than the increase in earnings and include increases for older children. To avoid incentive problems child benefit would need to grow by the same amount. That means increases in taxation on those who can afford to pay.

Politics is about choices. The British people are comparatively low taxed. Our tax system is only mildly redistributive. If child poverty is really the number one domestic priority then all resources should be used to speed up the anti-poverty strategy. There should be no further cuts in income tax until the Government's pledge is achieved – because it cannot be achieved without redistribution, without more taxing and more spending.

NOTES

1 Department of Social Security, *Households Below Average Income: a statistical analysis*, 1994/95–1998/99, The Stationery Office, 2000 (and earlier years)

2 Department of Social Security *Households Below Average Income 1979-1996/97*, Corporate Document Services, 1998

3 J Mack and S Lansley, *Poor Britain*, Allen and Unwin, 1985; G Gordon and C Pantazis, *Breadline Britain in the 1990s*, Ashgate, 1997

4 Gordon et al, *Poverty and Social Exclusion in Britain*, Joseph Rowntree Foundation, 2000

5 J Bradshaw (ed), *Poverty: the outcomes for children*, Family Policy Studies Centre, 2001

6 J Bradshaw, 'Child Poverty in Comparative Perspective', *Journal of European Social Security*, 1/4, 1999, pp383–404; B Bradbury and M Jantti, *Child Poverty Across Industrialised Countries*, Innocenti Occasional Paper, Economic and Social Policy Series, No 71, 1 UNICEF International Child Development Centre, 1999; UNICEF, *A League Table of Child Poverty in Rich Countries*, Innocenti Report Card 1, UNICEF, 2000; H Oxley, T Dang, M Forster and M Pellizzari, 'Income Inequalities and Poverty Among Children and Households with Children in Selected OECD: Trends and Determinants', Paper to the Luxembourg Income Survey Conference, *Child Well-being in Rich and Transition Countries*, 1999; Eurostat, 'Income Distribution and Poverty in the EU' in *Statistics in Focus: Population and Social Conditions*, vol 6, 1997

7 Interview in the *Independent on Sunday* with Tony Blair, 26 July 1996

8 It could also be argued that the changes introduced in 1988 as a result of the 1986 Social Security Act also cut the real value of the scale rates for some types of claimant but were concealed by changes in the structure of benefits.

9 See note 1, p175

10 A Atkinson, *Macroeconomics and Children*, Innocenti Occasional Paper 68, UNICEF, 1998

11 Department of Social Security, *The Changing Welfare State: Opportunity for All: tackling poverty and social exclusion: first annual report,* Cm 4455, The Stationery Office, 1999

12 D Piachaud and H Sutherland, *How Effective is the British Government's Attempt to Reduce Child Poverty?* CASE Paper 38, LSE/STICERD, 2000

13 H Sutherland, *The British Government's Attempt to Reduce Child Poverty: a Budget 2000 postscript*, Microsimulation Unit Research Note No 36, 2000

14 Department of Social Security, *The Changing Welfare State: Opportunity for All, One Year On: making a difference*, Cm 4865, The Stationery Office, 2000
15 See for example, note 5
16 See note 11
17 However there are still criticisms to be made of the indicators:
   Indicator 1: Worklessness is a cause of poverty and not an outcome of poverty. Further, it is not inevitably associated with poverty – if social protection systems were more generous than they are then workless households would not be poor. There are also still poor children living with parents who earn their poverty – in 1998/99 31 per cent of children living in households with incomes in the bottom quintile had an employed parent.
   Indicator 7: School exclusions affect only 0.16 per cent of pupils. There is also little evidence of an association between school exclusions and poverty.
   Indicator 8: Housing conditions is not particularly useful as it is only available every five years.
   Indicator 9: Accident admissions and the length of them are an input and might vary over time and in different geographical areas according to policy and treatment regimes. It might have been better to have chosen the child mortality rate due to accidents as a more precise indicator of serious accidents, not least because it appears to be more closely associated with poverty than injuries. Or to refine it even further it might have been better to have chosen child deaths from traffic accidents or accidents in the home which are the two most clearly associated with poverty.
   Indicator 10: This indicator is selected on the grounds that the number of school leavers with no recognised qualifications 'is the most powerful predictor of unemployment at age 21' (DSS 1999). It is an input measure – and one which does not take account of the fact that some of those not learning will be in employment. It is therefore of limited use as an indicator of *current* child poverty.
   Indicator 12: Reducing the teenage conception rate is an objective of the Social Exclusion Unit report, *Teenage Pregnancy* (1999). The conception rate includes those that eventually end in abortion, and abortion and access to abortion are policy inputs which can be manipulated. It is arguable that it would have been better to have selected the teenage birth rate, or the proportion of teenage pregnancies which end in births.
18 See note 14
19 See note 12
20 See note 13
21 A technique that seeks to adjust income to reflect the relative needs of different household compositions; see also note 9 of Chapter 5
22 H Parker (ed), *Low Cost but Acceptable: a minimum income standard for the UK: families with young children*, The Policy Press, 1998

2 Children's benefits and credits: is an integrated child credit the answer?

Martin Barnes and Geoff Fimister

The Government's initial over-emphasis on 'welfare to work' as the answer to all ills led some to fear that, as the working families' tax credit took centre stage, benefits for children whose parents were out of work would be neglected. The emphasis on means-testing also suggested that child benefit might suffer. In the event, these misgivings have not been borne out, as the Government has injected additional resources into all of these benefits and credits to one degree or another. In particular, child benefit has not – so far – been left out of the anti-poverty policy frame, and out-of-work as well as in-work means-tested benefits have been improved, including a rounding-up of younger children's rates to achieve alignment with those for older children. Thus, in his November 2000 pre-Budget report,[1] the Chancellor was able to boast that:

- there have been 'record increases in child benefit, with a 26 per cent real increase in the rate for the first child since 1997';
- means-tested benefit rates for children under 11 'have been increased by 72 per cent in real terms since 1997';
- families claiming working families' tax credit are receiving, on average, £30 a week more than under family credit.

Jonathan Bradshaw, on the other hand, points out in the previous chapter that the effects of cuts in lone parents' benefits have to be set against the above improvements – and CPAG's reservations concerning the future of child benefit are set out below. Moreover, these impressive percentages operate from a low base. For example, the April 2001 under-16 child's rate of income support (inclusive of child benefit) will still only be £31.45 per week. Nevertheless, the additional resources are real and – in respect of out-of-work benefits – unexpected, given the initial drift of policy in 1997.

A further unexpected development was the announcement in March 1999 of a children's tax credit, to be paid in respect of most children (being withdrawn only from earners paying income tax at the top rate). This replaces the married persons' and additional personal tax allowances and commences in April 2001. While welcoming additional resources for families with children, CPAG would rather have seen the money going into further increases in child benefit. Initially, the new credit was announced at a rate equivalent to £8.50 per week for most taxpayers, but in November 2000 the Chancellor announced a revised figure of £10 per week.

The children's tax credit, though, is most unusual in having both an increase and its abolition announced before its introduction. If current plans go ahead after the general election, a major shake-up of children's benefits and credits is scheduled for 2003. An 'integrated child credit' (ICC) is planned, with the aim of bringing together the different strands of support for children to create 'an integrated and seamless system of child financial support paid to the mother, building upon the foundation of universal child benefit'.[2]

The children's payments to be brought together are those within working families' tax credit, income support, jobseeker's allowance, the disabled person's tax credit and the new children's tax credit. There are also implications for the structure and administration of housing benefit and council tax benefit.

CPAG has supported the ICC proposal as a possible simplification of the system of support for children, and particularly as a potential means of securing significant additional resources for low-income families. However, our support is not without reservations; there are hazards as well as opportunities. The ICC could be a useful supplement to child benefit – or it could replace it. The ICC could be a significant administrative improvement compared with current arrangements – or it could be a mess. The ICC could channel more money to children in low-income families – but it could also be used as an excuse for harsher labour market discipline in respect of their parents. In this chapter (which is based on evidence which the authors gave to the House of Commons Social Security Committee on 22 November 2000) we probe these issues and make suggestions as to how the next government should proceed.

THE OBJECTIVES OF THE INTEGRATED CHILD CREDIT

The declared objectives of the ICC are:[3]

- a seamless and transparent system of support for children;
- a portable and secure income bridge spanning welfare and work;
- a common framework for assessment and payment;
- a system where all support for children (is) paid to the main carer;
- efficiency gains for the Government and reduced red tape for parents.

We support all of these objectives and believe that they are achievable. However, integration and simplification alone will not achieve the goal of ending child poverty. Central to that goal is the need to secure an adequate income for children. We therefore welcome the fact that one of the purposes of a 'seamless and transparent' system is described as 'facilitating public debate about the correct level of support in the context of the Government's aim to abolish child poverty within a generation'.[4]

We would suggest adding to the above objectives:

- maintaining and improving the value of universal child benefit;
- achieving an adequate income for children and their families, linked to minimum income standards;
- minimising the problems associated with means-tested benefits (in particular, improving take-up, reducing complexity, improving administration and tackling the poverty trap).

The ICC will be paid to people in and out of work. For those in work, the ICC will be complemented by an employment tax credit (working families' tax credit in its current form thus ceasing to exist).

The Treasury recognises that the ICC will be 'a major structural reform... posing a number of operational and policy challenges. A critical test will be whether the integration of child payments can be delivered efficiently and effectively.'[5]

As noted above, introduction of the ICC is scheduled to commence in 2003. Given the substantial nature of the change, planning will need to proceed at a brisk pace. Nevertheless, this should not be at the expense of adequate consultation with interested parties, including claimants themselves and organisations such as CPAG which have considerable experience of how both the structure and administration of benefits impact upon low-income families.

THE IMPORTANCE OF CHILD BENEFIT

CPAG believes that, if each generation fully accepted its responsibility for the health and well-being of the next, the system of financial support for children would be universal and not subject to means-testing – hence our long-standing conviction that the best way to provide financial support for children is through a substantial increase in child benefit.

Child benefit achieves all the stated objectives of the ICC. In particular, it is portable and secure, spanning non-employment and work; it is administratively efficient; it provides a transparent system of support; it is paid to the main carer; and it has a very high take-up rate. These objectives are achieved because child benefit is not means-tested and is built on recognition of the importance of supporting all children.

We recognise that the Government's intention is to tackle many of the problems and objections presented by the current system of means-tested support for children. Nevertheless, we believe that it is crucial that the importance of child benefit is acknowledged. In the context of the ICC, CPAG believes that:

- child benefit should continue significantly to be increased in real terms, and as a minimum should be uprated annually in such a way as to keep pace with improvements in the general standard of living of our society – that is, at least in line with earnings;
- child benefit should remain universal (ie, not means-tested), whether conventionally or via a 'taper' higher up the income scale. It should also remain untaxed for all families.

The Government has indicated that the ICC – like the employment tax credit – will be administered and delivered by the Inland Revenue.[6] Although the Government has stated that the ICC will 'build on' child benefit, it is as yet unclear whether or not the latter will be paid along with the ICC. If, at some future stage, the two were to be paid together, then the amount of child benefit would need to be identified clearly in any decision letter, notification or instrument of payment.

We remain concerned that the introduction of an integrated payment may be an obstacle to further real increases in the value of child benefit. The ICC may, moreover, provide a political and structural mechanism for future 'targeting' of child benefit. It is for this reason that CPAG has described the proposal for an ICC as a potential Trojan horse for more means-testing. There needs to be a clear commitment that the real value of child benefit will be at least maintained, to counter concerns that in future it may be allowed to 'wither on the vine'.

In this context, it may be worrying that the very welcome additional increase in the children's additions to means-tested benefits and credits announced in the March 2000 Budget (£4.35 a week from June or October 2000, depending on the benefit or credit) contrasted with a much smaller increase (35p, or 50p for the first child) announced for child benefit from April 2001. Moreover, the latter figures included the normal inflation uprating, which in practice means there will be no increase in real terms.

The Chancellor, in his 1998 Budget statement, set out two principles governing his approach to improving financial support for families with children: a 'substantial increase' in such support, provided 'in the fairest way'. There is a danger that fairness may become equated with income-based targeting. In his 1999 Budget statement, the Chancellor said that it was 'in fulfilment of these two principles that the children's tax credit will be tapered away for the higher earning family'. We do not share the view that income-based targeting of support for children necessarily equates with fairness, as it means that support for poor families with children is being financed in part by other families with children, rather than by taxpayers in general. In other words, childless taxpayers are not paying their fair share towards support of future generations, upon which society as a whole will depend for its continuation.

For the same reasons, CPAG remains opposed to the taxation of child benefit in any form. We welcome the fact that taxation is not currently proposed, but believe that such a course should explicitly be ruled out.

THE LEVEL AND STRUCTURE OF THE INTEGRATED CHILD CREDIT

The central objective should be to set the ICC at a level which (in combination with child benefit) guarantees that all children are lifted clear of poverty. (The latter of course cannot be achieved unless the overall level of family income is also addressed – see below).

Work undertaken for the Commission on Social Justice set out clearly the differences between the often-confused concepts of a poverty line (a level of income below which evidence shows people cannot, on average, participate in the mainstream of their society); a minimum income standard (a political yardstick against which to measure incomes, which ought not to be below the poverty line but could – as a matter of political choice – be above it); and benefit rates (which are what the Government has decided to pay).[7]

A minimum income standard for a given family structure should not be set below what current reliable evidence shows is the participatory poverty line for that family. Such a minimum income standard should be used as an income target (whether the family has a full-time worker or not) informing the setting of benefit rates.

Making sense of the appropriate level for the integrated child credit + child benefit (ICC+CB) thus requires the establishment of a minimum income standard for children. However, it is clearly unrealistic to suppose that, in practice, families will be able to budget for children's needs in isolation from the circumstances of the other members of the family. In other words, the ICC has to be seen as part of a strategy to tackle inadequate family incomes in general, or its aims will be undermined by the overall background of continuing family poverty. This means addressing the question of a minimum income standard for adults as well as children – an essential step in determining the thresholds at which the ICC should begin to be withdrawn for different family types.

Few informed commentators would dispute that incomes for large numbers of families, particularly where nobody is in full-time paid work, are insufficient to prevent poverty and social exclusion. Although the Government has made an important start in improving income levels for families with children, much more needs to be done. We understand that current modelling of the ICC has used existing benefit levels for illustrative purposes, but that 'no decisions have yet been taken about the level of the integrated child credit'.[8] On cost grounds, there may be a temptation to stick close to existing benefit rates, but this should be resisted if the ICC is to be a true anti-poverty initiative.

So at what level should the Government pitch the ICC+CB? The Family Budget Unit has done useful work in costing low-income budgets (see Chapter 1) but has erred very much on the side of caution. The Government's use of various percentages of average incomes to measure poverty tells us a good deal about inequality, but nothing about need.

John Veit-Wilson has argued that the Government:

> …needs to amass as much evidence as it can and see how far it points
> the same way. This is known as 'triangulation', where the use of a variety

of methods can help to establish if the findings hold robustly across methods...

He suggests:[9]

- population surveys '...to discover what society defines as necessities which no one should be without...and then by statistical analysis the household income levels at which people actually are deprived or excluded';
- public opinion surveys '...to discover the average disposable income levels which people report their households need to make ends meet';
- focus group research '...to discover what people see as the minimally decent levels of living and the disposable income levels at which they can be achieved';
- scientific budget studies;
- nutritional surveys;
- health surveys;
- the range of regular government surveys of household incomes and expenditures;
- educational surveys.

We accept that it is, in practice, easier to show when income levels are inadequate than it is to point to a definitive (and agreed) income standard. This is not to say, though, that lengthy research programmes are necessary before progress can be made. Given the political will and the various sources of information which are already available, it ought to be possible to move fairly quickly. We support Veit-Wilson's call for a joint working party of central government representatives and outside specialists to take this work forward. We would add that consultative mechanisms would also be needed to engage other social interests, not least those most directly affected – that is, people on low incomes.

A key issue for the structure of the ICC is its relationship to child benefit. It is often said, rather misleadingly, that claimants of working families' tax credit and disabled person's tax credit can 'keep' their child benefit, whereas it is deducted from other means-tested benefits. What in fact happens is that child benefit is taken into account when the tax credit rates are set, rather than afterwards as part of the individual assessment. An integrated child credit will need to follow one or the other route.

Given the public perception of unfairness about 'losing' child benefit when claims for income support and means-tested jobseeker's allowance are assessed, there is clearly something to be said for the working families' tax credit model. However, a reduction at the point of change in means-tested payments for children of income support and jobseeker's allowance claimants might be politically difficult, given that most people find the intricacies of the system baffling and the change might simply be seen as a cut. If sufficient resources could be found to boost these rates far enough to avoid a cash reduction at the point of change, then the tax credit model (taking child benefit into account when rates are initially set) would be the more comprehensible to the public. It would also be more in keeping with the idea of 'building on' child benefit.

We argued above that the combined level of ICC+CB should be set at a level sufficient to keep children out of poverty. Given also the superiority of child benefit over means-tested payments in terms of efficiency and effectiveness, we would also argue that the *proportion of the total* which consists of child benefit should be maximised and improved at each uprating whenever possible.

As regards the ICC taper, the Government envisages an initial relatively steep rate above the threshold, followed by a plateau, followed by a final tapering away at the top end of the range in line with the projected children's tax credit.[10] Obviously, in terms of supporting families on low – but not quite the lowest – incomes, the gradient of withdrawal at the bottom end will be of key importance.

It should also be noted that a minimum income standard for a family should include an element to permit saving or borrowing to meet the costs of essential items of furniture and household equipment. Unless and until we can be confident that benefit rates have reached such a standard, there will be a continuing need for a system of grants to meet this area of need. The questions of a minimum income standard and the ICC, therefore, also have to be seen in the context of the need to reform the deeply flawed social fund. There is also a further, related question of access to affordable sources of credit – which is often confused with, but is not the same as, the need for a system of grants.

SOME DETAILED ASPECTS OF STRUCTURE

Creating the ICC from the existing framework of (not always consistent) benefits and credits will raise a number of technical, but important, issues. We do not have space to set these out fully here (a more detailed briefing is available from CPAG[11]). The following is a list of issues needing attention, which CPAG has raised with officials and with the House of Commons Social Security Committee:

- The location of the *family premium* (CPAG argues that it should stay where it is – that is, it should not be spread out more thinly across a larger number of children because of the losses this would cause to the poorest).
- Provision for *disabled children* (CPAG argues for an enhanced rate of ICC).
- The approach to *ages and numbers of children* (CPAG supports 'rounding up' and has suggested that this might be considered for child benefit).
- Financial support for *pregnant women and very young children* (CPAG has proposed several improvements linked to the ICC).
- The rules for determining who has *responsibility for a child* (rationalisation is needed).
- The location of the *childcare credit* (CPAG suggests attaching it to the ICC).
- The rules for the *termination date* as the upper age limit for the ICC is reached (CPAG has flagged up the issue as regards the interface with the personal income entitlements of young people).
- Issues relating to *housing benefit and council tax benefit* (CPAG has raised a number of points concerning children's allowances in these schemes and the interaction of tax credit, housing benefit and council tax benefit withdrawal rates as income rises).
- Issues relating to *'passports'* (where arrangements need to be made to prevent the loss to many claimants of access to free school meals, health benefits, the social fund and the Sure Start maternity grant, as well as discounts and exemptions from charges under a variety of local authority schemes, as the ICC 'floats free' of the adult benefit).
- The future of the *children's additions to national insurance (and related) benefits* (CPAG has called on the Government to cease to implement its predecessor's long-standing policy of gradually phasing these out).
- The interface between the ICC and *residence, presence and immigration issues* (CPAG has called for policy to be based on the need to counter poverty and social exclusion).

ASSESSMENT OF RESOURCES

We would like to go into a certain amount of detail regarding the assessment of claimants' resources for the purpose of the ICC, as the

Government is clearly thinking hard about this and seems prepared to entertain significant simplification. The ICC thus offers an opportunity to get away from the obsessive complexity of the 'traditional' means-tested benefit. We would suggest that the following possibilities could be explored:

- Disregard all capital.
- Count only taxable income.
- Assess the ICC at six-monthly or annual intervals, with appropriate safeguards.

TREATMENT OF CAPITAL

The current means-tested benefits and credits take capital into account, although the children's tax credit will not. It will be necessary to decide which approach to adopt.

There is a strong case for ignoring capital in the assessment of the ICC – as the Government has decided to do for pensioners' benefits. The payment would be subject to assessment of taxable income (see below), including income derived from capital.

The need to collect information and adjudicate upon capital adds to the complexity of the assessment of means-tested benefits and credits. There are detailed questions on the application forms, proof is required from the claimant (eg, evidence of savings) and changes in capital held may require a review.

Within the present means-tested systems, all savings beneath a lower limit are ignored, while benefit is not payable above an upper limit. These limits vary from one context and/or benefit or credit to another. Between the two limits, benefit is reduced by £1 for every £250 above the lower threshold. Not only is this a complex set of formulae to understand, but the 'tariff' does not reflect a realistic rate of interest, being partly based on the assumption that there will be some depletion of capital (which in turn will require a reassessment of entitlement). There are also tortuous rules concerning notional capital, rate of assumed diminution of notional capital, capital treated as income, income treated as capital, etc etc.

We do not have detailed estimates, but common sense would suggest that significant administrative and time savings would follow from excluding these rules from the ICC, speeding up decision making and greatly reducing the scope for error and fraud.

Abolition of the capital rules in the context of the ICC would of course have a cost, but this could be relatively small, given that a high proportion of claimants with children (certainly as regards income support and jobseeker's allowance) have few or no savings. In light of this – and the proposed changes for pensioners – ignoring capital might not be such a radical step.

This approach, moreover, would be wholly consistent with the Government's observation that:

> The next phase of modernisation offers an opportunity for a thorough review of the treatment of income and capital... A modern system should be simple and aim to promote work, fairness and incentives to save.[12]

We indeed hope that such modernisation will see a substantial simplification of the remaining capital rules for *adult* benefits and credits.

If capital rules were abolished for the ICC while continuing within the other means-tested benefits and credits, it would of course be possible to be on a very low income and qualify for the former, but not for the latter. This would be, however, a relatively minor complication, well worth tolerating in exchange for the advantages outlined above.

TREATMENT OF INCOME

Greater simplification and efficiency savings would be achieved if the level of taxable income alone affected the ICC. This would simplify assessment, create greater transparency, reduce the scope for error and fraud and should generate administrative savings. It would again be consistent with the Government's objectives quoted above.

Modelling would of course be required to estimate the relative costs of different approaches, but the scope for streamlining structure and administration is attractive.

We would also hope that the ICC would follow the current tax credits in disregarding maintenance payments.

The period over which income is measured differs between the benefits and credits concerned, so decisions will need to be taken in respect of the ICC. It may well be that the method will vary depending on whether or not the claimant is in work. The aim should be to get as clear a reflection as possible of current circumstances (eg, last year's tax records would be unsuitable). Whatever approach is taken, we would emphasise the importance of the safeguards discussed below.

FREQUENCY OF ASSESSMENT

Given that adult means-tested benefits and credits will taper out first,[13] there will presumably be no need to re-assess the ICC itself (except in respect of changes in the number of children, or where a specific enhancement, for example because of a disability, is involved) as long as one of these is in payment.

Where assessment is needed, the question of frequency arises. We know from long experience that those benefits which are designed to respond to changes in circumstances on a weekly basis suffer enormous administrative problems where changes are frequent. This leads many claimants to fail to notify such changes (whether to their advantage or disadvantage) just to avoid 'the hassle'. Minor 'fraud' is often attributable to this factor, as is much underpayment.

There is, therefore, a strong case for assessing the ICC at intervals no more frequent than for tax credits – currently six months. The Government is also thinking along these lines; indeed, the recent Treasury paper makes out a case for annual awards.[14] It should be noted, however, that three safeguards would be needed:

1. Claimants would need to have the (well-publicised) right to ask for a review during the course of a claim, to avoid potential hardship. Given the effort involved, claimants are unlikely to seek reviews frivolously, so there would be no need to complicate matters with 'minimum changes of circumstances' rules; a simple right to ask for a review would suffice. This 'responsiveness' issue is recognised by the Treasury paper,[15] and has also been a feature of similar discussions around the review of housing benefit.[16]
2. The impending addition to the family of another child, once it becomes known to official agencies, should trigger an invitation to apply for a reassessment.
3. The rules relating to annual uprating of tax credits should be changed, the ICC following suit in due course, so that upratings are implemented each April, removing the present injustice whereby claimants risk potentially serious losses (and face tortuous 'better-off' calculations) if they become entitled (or aware of their entitlement) towards the end of the financial year. The longer the standard award period, the worse this problem is. Admittedly, if 1 above were accepted, knowledgeable claimants of ICC could solve the problem by applying for a review in order to access the new rate – but this would hardly be the way to run a transparent and efficient service.

SANCTIONS AND PENALTIES

The rules relating to benefit sanctions and penalties are complex and detailed, but their effect is either to eliminate or to reduce benefit, for various lengths of time, depending on circumstances and on which set of rules applies in a given case.

There are signs that the Government is not opposed to extending the element of compulsion within the benefit system. Compulsory 'work-related' interviews have been piloted and are being extended among groups (lone parents, sick or disabled people, carers) whose members are not required to seek work as a condition of entitlement. Ministers have spoken of extending New Deal benefit sanctions.

We presume that, like child benefit, the ICC will not be conditional upon a parent being available for and actively seeking work, attending work-related official interviews etc. Applying sanctions to money for a child in these circumstances would be directly contrary to the aim of promoting the well-being of children.

However, there is a danger that there may be a perception that, as the costs and needs of children are presumed to be met by a 'ring-fenced' ICC, other payments can be regarded as being solely to meet the expenses of adults in the family. The extension of sanctions against parents may, therefore, come to be perceived as politically more acceptable. In practice, however, as noted above, it is not realistic to treat the income needs of the family as neatly divisible between adults and children and such a development would in effect visit greater hardship upon the children concerned. The principle and practice of benefit sanctions require searching review, not extension.

DELIVERY

Whatever arrangements are made for the administration of the ICC, it is of course crucial that payment is made as quickly as possible. Reliable mechanisms must be in place for emergency payments if there are delays in the mainstream administration.

The Government envisages that the Inland Revenue will calculate and pay the ICC, but that it will be accessed via both the new agency for claimants of working age and the child benefit claims system (where a shared database is envisaged).

The recent Treasury document says that the new credits 'will aim to rely on electronic payment' but will 'take into account the needs of those who do not have a bank account'.[17] It is important, in terms of income distribution within the family, that the latter safeguard should include situations where the main carer in a couple does not have a separate bank account.

The Treasury document also observes that 'any new system developed by the Inland Revenue for the new tax credits (will require) close co-operation with other agencies and stakeholders'.[18] What is required, though, is rather more than co-operation; it is *integrated administration*. Adequate resources and lead-in times, with careful development and thorough testing of administrative and computer systems, are essential. The dismal history of housing benefit administration provides a sobering cautionary tale as regards the consequences of failing to observe these requirements in planning and running an inter-agency benefit system. These lessons must be taken seriously.

CONCLUSION

The proposed integrated child credit has considerable potential to contribute to the objective of abolishing child poverty. However, there are many structural and administrative complexities to be overcome and potential hazards to be circumvented.

What would be the fate of the plans for the ICC in the event of a change of government is not clear. It might be seen as a Labour project and dropped, or it might proceed in some form. Certainly, if the present government is returned, it would seem that the ICC is going to become a reality. The technical issues surrounding it should not be allowed to obscure the fact that here is a crucial issue for children and families.

NOTES

1 Chancellor of the Exchequer, *Building Long-Term Prosperity for All: pre-Budget report*, The Stationery Office, November 2000, paras 5.18-5.20

2 Chancellor of the Exchequer, *Budget Statement*, HM Treasury, 9 March 1999

3 HM Treasury, *The Modernisation of Britain's Tax and Benefit System: supporting children through the tax and benefit system*, November 1999, para 3.30; see also HM Treasury, *The Modernisation of Britain's Tax and Benefit System: tackling poverty and making work pay – tax credits for the 21st century*, March 2000, ch 2

4 HM Treasury, *The Modernisation of Britain's Tax and Benefit System: supporting*

children through the tax and benefit system, November 1999, para 3.30

5 See note 4, para 3.32

6 HM Treasury, *The Modernisation of Britain's Tax and Benefit System: tackling poverty and making work pay – tax credits for the 21st century*, March 2000, para 2.29

7 J Veit-Wilson, *Dignity Not Poverty: a minimum income standard for the UK*, Commission on Social Justice/Institute for Public Policy Research, 1994; see also (by the same author) *Setting Adequacy Standards: how governments define minimum incomes*, The Policy Press, 1998; and 'Setting a Governmental Minimum Income Standard – the next steps', *Poverty* 105, CPAG

8 See note 6, para 2.27

9 J Veit-Wilson, 'Setting a Governmental Minimum Income Standard – the next steps', *Poverty* 105, CPAG

10 See note 6, para 2.27

11 M Barnes and G Fimister, *The Integrated Child Credit: a briefing*, CPAG, October 2000

12 See note 6, para 4.15

13 See note 6, para 4.12

14 See note 6, paras 4.9-4.11

15 See note 6, paras 4.10-4.11

16 For example, Department of Social Security/Local Authority Association, *Housing Benefit Simplification and Improvement Project*, unpublished papers, 1999; Department of the Environment, Transport and the Regions and Department of Social Security, *Quality and Choice: a decent home for all – the housing Green Paper*, April 2000, para 11.26; House of Commons Social Security Committee, *Housing Benefit*, Sixth Report of Session 1999-2000, vol 1, paras 28-29

17 See note 6, para 4.19

18 See note 6, para 4.18

3 Employment and poverty

Richard Exell

The Government believes that joblessness is the most important cause of poverty, and helping more people into employment is at the centre of its anti-poverty strategy.[1] Ministers and officials would certainly argue that the labour market policies discussed in this chapter are every bit as important as benefit reforms to the future of poverty.

These policies have to be seen in context. Whatever else they are, employment programmes are always a response to what is happening in the labour market when they are designed. Most important labour market trends were well established by the time of the last general election:

- More people are in employment – between 1984 and 1999 the number of people in work grew by nearly three million.[2]
- Unemployment has been falling since 1993, and claimant count unemployment may fall below a million by the time of the next election.[3]
- The 1980s and 1990s saw women with younger dependent children become much more likely to be in employment, and women employees accounted for 45 per cent of the workforce by 1999.[4]
- But this change only benefited mothers with working partners. The proportion of lone parents in employment has fallen from about half in 1979[5] to 45 per cent now.[6] Women with unemployed partners have also lost out – 72.5 per cent of mothers with working partners are in employment, compared with 35.3 per cent of those with non-working partners.[7]
- Pay has become more unequal. In 1979, the wages of the top 10 per

cent of full-time male employees were about 2.4 times greater than the wages of men in the bottom 10 per cent. For women, the ratio was about 2.1. By 1999 (before the introduction of the national minimum wage) these ratios had increased to 3.4 for men, and 3.1 for women.[8]

• Joblessness is not just about unemployment – in addition to unemployed people, there are those who are 'economically inactive' (neither employed nor unemployed) who, when asked, say they would like a job. Altogether, there were 3.9 million people in these two groups in November 2000 – more than 10 per cent of the working-age population.[9]

The Government's active labour market policy follows on from its interpretation of these trends: the economy is creating the jobs that will help people to escape poverty, but some people are much less successful than others at getting these jobs. As the Department for Education and Employment has put it:

> Britain is working. There are over one million more people in work than in Spring 1997. With unemployment falling, and low inflation, that means rising living standards across Britain. There are record numbers of people in work...But there is still much more to do. Unemployment is still too high. Pockets of very high unemployment remain; within every region there are big variations between the most and least successful areas.[10]

This interpretation of the labour market explains why the new policies introduced since 1997 are not designed to create jobs, so much as to influence who gets them and how well off they are in them.

HELPING PEOPLE INTO WORK

One of the 'big picture' decisions the Government got right early on was targeting joblessness, rather than unemployment. Families with no one in a job tend to be poor, even when none of the family members receives jobseeker's allowance; and many lone parents, disabled people and involuntarily early-retired workers would like a job if they thought there was a realistic chance of getting one.

But public policy has been slow to recognise this. The Employment Service only helped people receiving jobseeker's allowance and the delivery of other benefits was divorced from the delivery of labour market programmes. Those programmes seemed to have been designed more as hurdles to discourage people from claiming jobseeker's allowance than as genuine routes back to work, and, for some years, claimants were actively encouraged to switch from unemployment to invalidity benefit.

This is changing. Since the 1998 publication of *The Way Ahead for the Employment Service*, delivering services to a wider range of benefit recipients – including lone parents and disabled people – has been a key new direction.[11] Since 1999, in a dozen areas, the pilots for the new ONE service have brought together the various agencies delivering benefits and employment services in a one-stop approach. Since April 2000 people living in a pilot area who claim a ONE benefit[12] have been required to attend a work-focused interview with a personal adviser.

This integrated approach is due for a major extension later this year, when the Employment Service will be merged with those elements of the Benefits Agency that work with people of working age to create a new 'Working Age Agency'. Very few details of the new agency had been announced as this chapter was written, though the Prime Minister's announcement promised that it will be 'equipped with the latest technology and located in high streets and town centres throughout the country…information on job vacancies, training, services and benefits as well as childcare will all be available at the touch of a button'.[13] This is a laudable vision, especially given the difficulties there will be in merging two massive agencies with radically different organisational cultures.

While organisational change may be important in the long term, it is the new programmes the Government has introduced that have attracted most attention. There is no shortage of these: there are employment zones, job action teams, job grants and the Job Transition Service for areas hit by large-scale redundancies.

But all of these are, of course, overshadowed by the New Deal. Strictly speaking, one should always talk about the New Deals, remembering the programmes for older long-term unemployed people, lone parents, disabled people, partners of the unemployed and for people over 50.

The Government's recognition that there is a problem about who gets the jobs the economy is creating has led to the establishment of special New Deals for the groups seen as facing the worst problems. Most of this investment has been directed at young people – despite a substantial fall in youth unemployment, £1 billion will have been spent on this programme by April 2001, compared with £520 million on all the other New Deals combined.[14] The Government has justified this on the grounds that the overwhelming priority is to prevent the emergence of a generation cut off from the rest of society.

There is a lot to be said for this argument, but it is undeniable that, objectively speaking, other groups face worse obstacles. A higher proportion of older long-term unemployed people, for instance, have no qualifications at all, and the discrimination faced by unemployed disabled people is worse than that faced by young unemployed people. It is time for these groups to catch up.

INDIVIDUALISATION AND COMPULSION IN LABOUR MARKET POLICY

It is impossible to think about the New Deals without responding to two themes of the Government's active labour market policy which we have already seen illustrated by the ONE project: the individualisation of support and the continued use of compulsion.

One of the worst features of past active labour market programmes was the sausage machine approach. A single model of what unemployed people needed was applied to everyone, with no attempt to identify the problems faced by the individual unemployed person, who was forced to take part by benefit penalties. Given the fact that they had a captive market, it is not surprising that the quality of most of these schemes was low, and unemployed people tended to regard them as their punishment for having the temerity to claim benefit.

With the new programmes the Government has made real progress towards treating unemployed people as individuals, but at the same time it has retained the threat of benefit penalties for those who do not take part. The personal adviser service offered by ONE, the New Deal programmes, employment zones and the Job Transition Service does mark something genuinely new in British labour market policy. At their best, personal advisers work *with* their clients, addressing the whole range of problems that can hinder their getting back to work. Everyone who has assessed these programmes has come the conclusion that the quality of the personal advisers is vital to success or failure, and we can reasonably expect to see extra resources for these advisers featuring in any increase in public spending under a Labour government. The Conservatives have not highlighted personal advisers in their blanket dismissal of the programmes introduced since 1997, but their promise to abolish the New Deal suggests that this approach would come to a sudden end under a Hague government.

The Government has continued the use of benefit penalties to require participation in the New Deals for older long-term unemployed people and young people. The main programme is famous for having 'no fifth option' of refusing to participate while claiming benefit and many people have been willing to accept that penalties are fair as long as participants have a genuine choice of four options. But even those of us who have accepted this have been dismayed as the Government has introduced the toughest benefit penalties ever faced by British unemployed people, with young unemployed people who break the New Deal rules for a third time facing a benefit suspension lasting six months.

More benefit sanctions are being imposed on claimants. In the New Deal for young people's first full year (from 1 April 1998 to 31 March 1999) 8,030 jobseeker's allowance sanctions were imposed for questions relating to a New Deal option. By 1999–2000, this had risen to 18,764. Ominously, the biggest category of reasons for sanctions was failure to attend an environment task force place – one sanction in five was applied to a young person who had voted with his or her feet against the programme's weakest option.[15]

There has been a general trend to require more people to look for work and take part in labour market programmes. Already, in the ONE pilots, widows and disabled people are, for the first time, required to attend an initial work-focused interview. Across the country, from 2001:

- lone parents with children over five will have to attend an initial work-focused interview;
- new 'joint claiming' rules for jobseeker's allowance will apply the full range of labour market eligibility conditions to the partners of unemployed people if they were born after 1976 and do not have children;
- the New Deal for older long-term unemployed people will be compulsory, and backed up with the same 'three strikes and you're out' rule as the main programme.

But policy is not set in stone. When the New Deal for people over 25 is reformed in 2001 it will consist of an initial Gateway, followed by an 'intensive activity period' of up to six months. This second element of the programme will normally be compulsory – but for people aged over 50 it will be voluntary. Exempting the over-50s from labour market obligations is a new development, and seems to be based on the Government's perception that applying the compulsory regime to this age group would be demeaning to them.

In other words, there are still debates which can be won about where the boundary lies between who should be *required* to look for work, and who should be *helped*. The continuing wrangle about the balance between mothers' and fathers' roles in their families and the workplace will have a practical impact on decisions in this area of policy, as will public perceptions of disabled and unemployed people.

Talking to people who deliver the New Deal, one of the messages that comes across is that more unemployed people than was expected have multiple problems: unemployment *and* homelessness, or unemployment *and* addiction, for instance. They need jobs, but the most realistic route to those jobs may well be to address their other problems first. The Government's new emphasis on individualised support for unemployed people is an important step towards helping, but it is likely to be undermined by benefit coercion.

THE NATIONAL MINIMUM WAGE

Policy has had to respond to the massive increase in earnings inequality over the last 20 years. The Government would have little to boast about if, after much effort, it succeeded in getting the most socially excluded people into jobs, but they were still poor at the end of it all.

The Government's strategy for dealing with low pay combines the introduction of the tax credits and higher child benefit (dealt with in other chapters) with the national minimum wage. The introduction of the minimum wage in April 1999 raised the incomes of 1.5 million workers, two-thirds of them women. What is more, it did this without any of the disasters predicted by critics:

- Remember the predictions that millions of jobs were at risk? *Employment rose by a quarter of a million* in the minimum wage's first year.
- Remember the threat to the competitiveness of British firms? The minimum wage raised the national wage bill by *0.5%.*
- Remember how inflation was going rocket? Price rises in 1999 were *less than half* the level of the year before.[16]

The national minimum wage has been so successful that even the Conservative Party has dropped the threat to abolish it – though whether a Hague government would ever uprate it is another matter.

It is plain now that the main problem with the minimum wage is that it is too low:

- The minimum wage does not apply to workers aged under 18.
- For workers aged over 18 and under 22, the youth rate of **£3.20** applies.
- For workers aged 22 and over who are on an accredited training course there is a 'development rate' of **£3.20**.
- For other workers aged 22 and over the minimum wage is **£3.70**.

There is no fair reason why someone over 21 should get a higher rate of pay than their younger colleague for doing the same work – or why a 16 or 17-year-old doing the same job is not covered by the minimum wage at all. What is more, these rates are ineffective because they are not high enough to protect workers from poverty, even when they have full-time jobs. The trouble-free introduction of the minimum wage suggests that it could be raised to somewhere between £4.50 and £5 without any damage to the economy.

Finally, the minimum wage should be updated regularly. Irregular uprating leads to low-paid workers continually falling behind the rest of the workforce, and ensures repeated protracted battles over each uprating. Regular upratings, by contrast, should help make the discussions about the next increase in the minimum wage an uncontroversial part of normal wage setting.

CONCLUSION

If we look at what has happened in the world of work, we see real advances and real problems. The minimum wage will make a real difference to the lives of thousands of low-paid workers – but it would make an even bigger difference if it were set at a higher level and uprated regularly. In the New Deal one recognises the investment in unemployed people that for years has been a key campaigning objective – but using benefit penalties to force unemployed people to participate could undermine its effectiveness. These issues have not yet been finally decided, and the end result may depend on seemingly theoretical debates about paid and unpaid work, and about who has a duty to work and who has a right to it.

NOTES

1 See for instance, any of HM Treasury's *Modernisation of Britain's Tax and Benefit System* series, or *Tackling Poverty and Extending Opportunity*, 1999
2 *Labour Force Survey*, historical supplement
3 *Labour Force Survey*, November 2000
4 See note 2
5 Department of Social Security, *Women and Social Security*, 1998
6 Speech by the Chancellor of the Exchequer to the Child Poverty Action Group conference on child poverty, 15 May 2000
7 HM Treasury, *Tackling Poverty and Extending Opportunity*, 1999
8 *New Earnings Survey*, April 1999 – ie, just before the introduction of the national minimum wage
9 *Labour Force Survey* data; it is worth remembering that this figure is coming down too, having stood at 4.5 million in the summer of 1997 (2,058,000 ILO unemployed and 2,401,000 million economically inactive people wanting work)
10 Department for Education and Employment, *Employment Now*, 2000, p1
11 See note 10, pp 4 and 6
12 Income support, incapacity benefit, severe disablement allowance, housing benefit, council tax benefit, jobseeker's allowance and widows' benefits
13 Department of Social Security, Press Release 2000/070, 16 March 2000
14 HM Treasury, *Pre-Budget Report*, November 2000
15 Employment Service, *Analysis of Adjudication Officers' Decisions*, 1999, p3; Employment Service, *Analysis of Sector Decision Making*, 2000, p3
16 Introduction to the *Second Report* of the Low Pay Commission, 2000

4 Excellence, diversity and inequality in education

George Smith and Teresa Smith

BACKGROUND

Education and educational reform were at the centre of the 1997 general election campaign. Tony Blair explicitly placed education as his 'number one' priority for Labour and in his major set piece speech on education in Birmingham, just before the election, set out 21 promises, ranging from a guaranteed nursery place for all four- year-olds, through cutting class sizes to 30 or fewer at Key Stage 1 (age five to seven), to making the Department for Education and Employment (DfEE) a leading office of state. This focus and priority has been maintained throughout the ensuing period of government, with both Blair and Secretary of State, David Blunkett regularly reaffirming the centrality of education to their overall strategy. Indeed, Tim Brighouse[1] picks out an additional six major educational initiatives to add to these 21 initial promises. Education, particularly further reform of secondary schooling, seems certain to be at the centre of Labour's forthcoming election campaign.

In this short review of what has happened since 1997 we focus predominantly on school and pre-school rather than higher or further education and, as far as possible, on the impact on children from low-income families and socially disadvantaged areas. Space limits the story effectively to England. We should be clear at the outset that much of the data available reflects, at best, only the first three years of this administration. It may be that many of the initiatives have gathered pace since then, particularly once the tough overall constraints imposed on government spending began to be eased in 2000. But with the priority explicitly given to education and the goal of using education to tackle poverty and social disadvantage through increased opportunities, it is reasonable to ask how it has worked out so far. How far have the priorities been translated into results on the ground?

THE INHERITANCE

It is worth briefly recalling the position in 1997 so that we can carry forward the story to 2001. A decade of education reform since the 1986 and 1988 Education Acts had effectively reshaped the school system in England, with a much higher degree of centralisation of power at the DfEE, but also decentralisation of responsibility to individual schools (and by extension, to parents and pupils) to deliver the results. The watchwords (set out in *Choice and Diversity*[2]) were for 'quality' to be delivered through more effective schools, following the National Curriculum; 'diversity' achieved through schools opting out of local authority control, the Assisted Places Scheme and other initiatives; 'parental choice' and 'greater school autonomy' through the local management of schools; and 'greater accountability' through published league tables of pupil performance and the four-year cycle of school inspection by the Office for Standards in Education (OFSTED). Whether all this, in fact, amounted to a 'quasi market' where parents could shop around for a school of their choice remains in doubt. For most, there was no real choice. And it is worth recalling that in the final stages of the Major administration there were moves to increase schools' powers to select children. Such selection shifts the power of choice from parents to schools.

Paradoxically perhaps, this period of intense reform in education was also a time when educational results, measured by examination success, increased significantly. Those getting five or more GCSE/GNVQ A*–C grades grew from 33 per cent in 1988/89 to 45 per cent in 1996/97; those getting two or more A levels from 17.3 per cent of the age group in 1988/89 to 29.2 per cent in 1996/97. These figures have continued to increase under the new administration, with the proportion attaining five or more GCSE/GNVQ A*–C grades reaching 49 per cent of the age group in 1999/2000. Numbers in higher education have also continued to grow.

During the 1990s concern for the apparently widening gulf between advantaged and disadvantaged areas, schools and pupils began increasingly to feature in educational debate (for example, the HMI/

OFSTED report, *Access and Achievement in Urban Education*[3]). These trends undoubtedly reflected the underlying social and economic polarisation as poverty, and particularly child poverty, became more acute. By the mid 1990s more than half of all children aged under 16 in the five poorest local education authorities (LEAs) in England (in London and the North West) were living in families dependent on the basic means-tested benefit, income support. The figure for England as a whole in 1995 was about 25 per cent. But any response in education was still at the margins of policy, and likely to be in the form of further public exposure of the apparent failure of local authorities or schools in disadvantaged areas to deliver (for example, in the 1996 OFSTED study of reading performance in three London boroughs, all of which were in the ten highest LEAs in England in terms of the proportion of children living in families receiving income support[4]).

LABOUR'S REFORMS

In one sense all this has changed dramatically under the new administration. There is now a raft of new policies and initiatives designed to tackle the problems of disadvantaged areas, schools and pupils (set out in more detail below). What was marginal has become of central concern, reflected in the increased availability of statistics, findings and recommendations for further action, including the high profile output from the Cabinet Office's Social Exclusion Unit. Thus, in addition to its earlier reports, *Truancy and School Exclusion*[5] and *Bridging the Gap: new opportunities for 16–18-year-olds not in education, employment or training*[6], at least three of the agenda-setting Policy Action Team (PAT) reports (that grew out of the major Social Exclusion Unit report, *Bringing People Together*[7]) focused on education or related topics (PAT 2: *Skills*[8]; PAT 11: *Schools Plus*[9]; and PAT 12: *Youth*[10]). There is also a new-found willingness to commission formal evaluations of these developments, so we will be in a better position to know 'what works'.

But there have been some surprising continuities in educational policy and reform. The new administration moved quickly to wind up programmes such as the Assisted Places Scheme and educational vouchers for four-year-olds, but it has taken over much of the package of educational reforms and apparatus created since the late 1980s, though subtly redefining and reshaping their purpose. We can group these changes into three types. First would come the general direction and purpose of educational change under the new government; second would be policies designed to increase the effectiveness of the present system and finally changes of a more 'structural' nature which either supplement or replace existing arrangements.

EDUCATIONAL GOALS

Of the five 'great themes' in the 1992 White Paper (*Choice and Diversity*[11]) most find an echo in the new programme. 'Excellence and diversity' are now the key ideas – 'diversity' particularly being endorsed and actively pursued at secondary level by the creation of more 'specialist' schools (in technology, languages, sports and arts) and the designation of 'beacon' schools of excellence to work with others to share their skills. This move to specialist schools forms one of the principal policy strands in the Excellence in Cities programme aimed at disadvantaged urban areas. There is also diversity in provision through the extension of the voluntary aided sector to include other religious groups (Muslim, Sikh, Seventh Day Adventist). But this diversity is to be set within a comprehensive secondary school framework – 'diversity underpinned by co-operative working so that diversity builds an effective education system, not just some effective schools.'[12] This meets the main objection to the emphasis on 'diversity' under the previous government – that it was a route to individual school success at the expense of others. The consistent analysis that runs through both Blunkett and Blair's pronouncements is of a much more individualised education and employment future (individual 'car journeys' rather than mass transit by train or bus of the past), and hence the need for an individually tailored and diverse education system. The yet to be resolved question is whether such diversity can be delivered without creating gainers and losers, and whether 'parity of esteem' can be achieved by different forms of education. The history of English secondary education is not encouraging, with its tendency to develop clear 'pecking orders', though systems in some other countries have been more successful in creating parallel and equally valued tracks. If this can be achieved, it will be a notable success.

GETTING MORE OUT OF THE EXISTING SYSTEM

Another key element inherited from the previous administration was the mechanism to lever higher performance out of the existing system. A strong line on 'poverty – no excuse' was maintained as forcefully as under the previous government. The apparatus for league tables of national curriculum assessments and examination results, for published inspection reports and lists of 'failing schools' on 'special measures' all continued effectively unchanged until the end of 2000. Then the resignation of Chris Woodhead, Chief Inspector of Schools in England and head of OFSTED, perhaps symbolically put an end – at least temporarily – to this phase of 'name and shame' and the central inquisitor's role he had prominently played under both Conservative and Labour administrations. These methods of driving up standards by the use of stick rather than carrot may well have helped take up the initial slack in the system; it would certainly be difficult to argue that they had no effect. Such methods, however, are time-limited and likely to be counter-productive, particularly in disadvantaged areas where national standards are much harder to achieve. Little or no allowance was made for these background conditions in judging a school's results. Yet at a time of economic buoyancy nobody is forced to take a teaching post, especially not in a difficult school or area. Teaching shortages and teacher turnover, particularly in urban areas, returned unwelcomed to the policy agenda.

This initially tough line on schools was exacerbated by the exceedingly tough expenditure constraints on education spending in the first two to three years of the new administration. There are clear signs now of moves to both a more relaxed spending regime following the Autumn 2000 spending package and a more subtle and sympathetic approach to motivating schools and teachers.

STRUCTURAL REFORMS

This last category is where there has been the clearest break from the past, with a number of significant developments. Simply to list and briefly describe these initiatives would take the rest of this chapter. Indeed one criticism might be the confusing array of often attractively, but unhelpfully, named programmes that have been set up. Who, but a closely involved professional, could reliably distinguish between Head Start, Sure Start, New Start, Fresh Start, Home Start? There are now welcome moves to combine and restructure these programmes into broader initiatives. Thus, the major Excellence in Cities programme, targeted at disadvantaged urban areas, pulls together under one heading seven different initiatives or 'policy strands' (specialist schools, beacon schools, educational action zones, learning mentors, gifted and talented programmes for the most able, city learning centres and learning support units).

PRE-SCHOOLING

Pre-schooling reforms may not yet amount to the radical and coherent approach to early childhood education that critics argue for. However, this age group has had a central place in the Government's programme since the 1997 election[13] and the Government's explicit commitment to ending child poverty has given clear priority to the most disadvantaged families and areas. First, there has been a significant expansion of provision for the under-fives, targeting the most disadvantaged. In 1998 the new government launched a national childcare strategy, the Green Paper, *Meeting the Childcare Challenge*, and the Comprehensive Spending Review White Paper which announced significant new funding for the under-fives, including the £540 million plans for Sure Start, offering integrated area-based health, education and welfare provision to 0–3-year-olds in disadvantaged areas. The number of Sure Start projects will double to 500 by 2004 – but even so, only one third of disadvantaged 0–3-year-olds will have access to this programme. In addition, all four-year-olds are guaranteed a free early education place, in either local authority services or accredited voluntary or private provision through the nursery education grant: in some local authorities take-up is virtually 100 per cent. Two-thirds of three-year-olds will have a place by 2002, with priority funding for areas of greatest social need, according to the Government's second annual poverty report; so far, 83,000 places have been created.

Second, a more coherent approach is developing to provision for this age group, formerly split between 'education' or 'care', with the Government's commitment to 'delivering integrated, comprehensive early education and childcare'. Early years development and childcare partnerships bring together all 'stakeholders' in early years, from the largest local authority and health authority to individual childminders. For the first time, authorities are required to review their services through the annual childcare audits and early years development plans. All services have been brought under the 'education' banner at local authority level. There is a common system of accreditation and inspection, now under OFSTED. There are moves towards common funding. Most importantly, there is a common educational framework with the beginning of the 'foundation stage' at age three, and the introduction of the 'early learning goals' and curriculum to all early years services funded by the nursery grant. But there is still a long way to go before all young children have equal access to high quality, integrated and comprehensive services.

SCHOOL LEVEL

The thrust of school level reforms to tackle poverty and inequality has been to increase opportunities – better qualifications leading to more secure and better paid employment in the future. Hence the stress on literacy and numeracy progress through 'literacy hours' and daily maths lessons in the primary phase, on reducing truancy and school exclusion at secondary level, on resources for more effective schooling through school improvement grants, and the piloting of educational maintenance allowances to retain young people from disadvantaged backgrounds in education above the minimum age. This stress on increasing opportunity through education perhaps can draw attention to the interdependence of education and social factors. Thus, one very effective way of improving educational results stems from improving the underling social and economic environment, rather than relying on education on its own.

AREA-BASED PROGRAMMES

Labour revived the idea of area-based programmes to target educational disadvantage. The argument is that this approach goes beyond individual schools. The first example was the educational action zones, of which there are more than 70 different local projects run by small consortia of ad hoc groups representing local schools, local business and other organisations. This initiative has been overtaken by the subsequent Excellence in Cities programme that rolls together many existing initiatives, including the newly announced 'small educational action zones'. In addition to the question of the purpose and effectiveness of the business element in these initiatives, there is also the question of the formal accountability of the ad hoc local structures formed to deliver these and other local programmes.[14]

WHAT ARE THE RESULTS SO FAR?

Many of the programmes and changes we have briefly reviewed are in their early stages. Though the Government has commissioned evaluations of many of these, it is too soon to report how they have worked out. It is already possible, however, to chart some of the general directions in the regular statistics made available by the DfEE.

First, in terms of expenditure it was probably only in the third year (1999/2000) that educational expenditure at school level began to rise in real terms.[15] Indeed, in the first two years expenditure per pupil was more or less steady at primary level from the early 1990s at £1,900 per pupil, and actually fell in real terms at secondary level (from £2,700 in 1992/93 to about £2,500 in 1998/99). If education was the priority, this was not reflected in any dramatic changes in spending. All this began to change from 2000 onwards, but as yet we do not have the outcome figures for this period.

Second, as Brighouse[16] notes, there has been significant progress on the specific commitments made at the outset and their subsequent additions. Thus, there was substantial progress in the reduction of class sizes over 30 at Key Stage 1. By January 2000 approximately 90 per cent of classes at this level had 30 or fewer pupils – up from about three-quarters in 1997. However, the position at Key Stage 2 was virtually unchanged, with consistently 30 per cent of classes at this level with 31 or more pupils, and at secondary level the pupil teacher ratio actually grew marginally worse. It should be pointed out that improvement in this respect – worthwhile in its own right – would have had very little impact on disadvantaged areas. These areas were already likely to have much smaller classes at this level. Thus, in Inner London in 2000 about 95 per cent of all Key Stage 1 classes had 30 pupils or less.[17]

Other statistics show some significant changes, but it is as yet difficult to attribute these to the changing programmes. Thus, the number of permanent exclusions fell from over 12,000 pupils in 1996/97 to just over 10,000. While exclusions for Black Caribbean pupils remained substantially higher than average, the number fell back slightly more rapidly. But parental appeals over their school choices continued to rise steeply with nearly 86,000 appeals at primary and secondary level in 1998/99. This may reflect increased parental familiarity with the appeals procedure and willingness to use it, but suggests that once the genie of 'parental choice' was released, it will continue to have a major impact on the shape of the school system.

But what of the more fundamental inequalities between disadvantaged groups and areas and the rest of the population in terms of educational progress and outcomes? These have proved intractable over many years and appeared to be widening during the late 1980s and first half of the 1990s. Certainly longer term studies of educational inequality by gender, race and social class suggest that there have been substantial reductions in gender inequalities and some reduction in inequalities among ethnic groups.[18] But differences by social back-

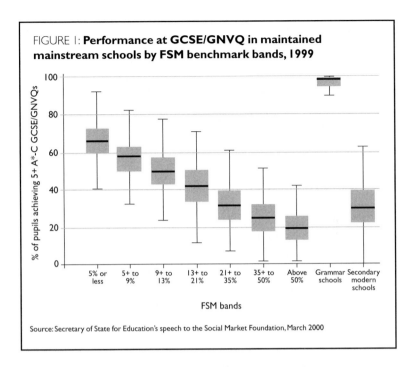

FIGURE 1: **Performance at GCSE/GNVQ in maintained mainstream schools by FSM benchmark bands, 1999**

FSM bands

Source: Secretary of State for Education's speech to the Social Market Foundation, March 2000

ground have remained relatively unchanged.

Figure 1, drawn from a presentation by the Secretary of State on transforming secondary education, underlines the sharpness of the problem. The examination data is for a single year (1999). The first seven box plots represent the GCSE/GNVQ performance of secondary schools grouped by the proportion of their pupils receiving free school meals. The solid bar in each box represents the average for each set of schools; the box represents the 50 per cent of schools around the average and the longer vertical line the range of schools. The pattern is clear. Schools with 5 per cent or fewer of their pupils on free schools meals get more than 60 per cent of their pupils to five or more GCSE/GNVQ grades A*–C, while the figure for schools where 50 per cent or more of pupils receive free school meals averages about 20 per cent. The two boxes to the right-hand side represent the 166 remaining grammar schools with typically almost all their pupils getting five or more A*–C grades and the 153 remaining secondary modern schools with a much lower level of performance. The figure, in effect, clearly represents the two alternative forms of secondary education; of selection by ability, which produces two completely separate distributions; or the more variable effect of neighbourhood and social background.

Finally we can ask about the trends in performance at secondary level over this period. In Figure 2 we have used the GCSE results for LEAs over the period 1996/97–1999/2000 (provisional data). Using the same criteria of the proportion of pupils getting five or more A★–C grade results the LEAs have been grouped into five bands based on the proportion of their under-16 population living in families getting income support or income-based jobseeker's allowance in 1998. In the poorest 20 per cent of LEAs 37 per cent or more of their under-16s are in this category. In the better off LEAs it is under 12 per cent. While there are problems in consistency (many new LEAs were formed as new unitary authorities over this period) the pattern appears to be relatively clear. First the effects of social and economic background are seen in the relative positions. Poorer areas have success rates in the 30-35 per cent range, whereas better off areas are pushing towards 55 per cent of the age group to this level of GCSE. It should be underlined that these are averages. Children from poor homes are not destined to be educational failures; it is just more likely that they will do less well than their counterparts from more advantaged areas. But second, in Figure 2, all groups moved ahead more or less in parallel over the period (1997-2000). Though this may look a disappointing result, results for earlier years suggest if anything a divergence with better off areas gaining qualifications more rapidly. Thus, not to fall further behind could be quite a positive finding. Of course, changes other than in education could be partially responsible. There was certainly a reduction in child poverty over this period in terms of the proportion of children living in families dependent on income support or jobseeker's allowance (down from 25 per cent in 1995 to 21 per cent in 1998).

CONCLUSION

It is too soon to say how effective the Labour administration has been overall with its educational programme. Certainly for the first time in many years we have had a government with a firm commitment to reduce educational inequality and the willingness to compile reports and statistics that fully chart what needs to be done. It is clear that there has been progress on many of the explicit objectives set out at the start, particularly where these have had a clear mechanism by which they could be achieved (for example, the commitment to reduce class size). There are also a very large number of programmes that have as their

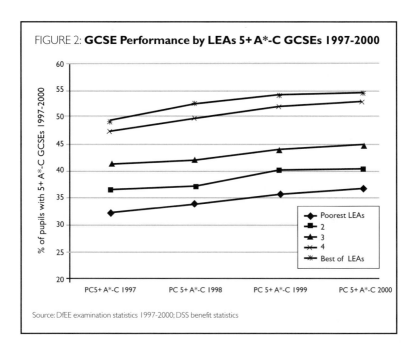

FIGURE 2: **GCSE Performance by LEAs 5+A*-C GCSEs 1997-2000**

Source: DfEE examination statistics 1997-2000; DSS benefit statistics

explicit purpose the improvements of educational opportunities in disadvantaged areas. It remains as yet unclear how the objectives of increasing diversity fit with the objectives of widening opportunity. But in terms of results at age 16 there is some suggestion that at least gaps have not widened further.

By firmly linking itself to a tight financial policy in the first two to three years the Government certainly gave itself a much harder job to promote its educational priorities. By continuing with a large part of the policies of the previous government to press for more out of the system, it has, perhaps, also critically reduced the support and goodwill it needed from the educational system if it is to deliver more. All this may have changed in the final year as financial constraints were at least temporarily relaxed, and a noticeably more co-operative climate developed. Two issues remain – first, the importance of consolidating and systematising the rash of initiatives aiming to tackle educational disadvantage, and second, the resolution of the necessary intermediate institutions between central government and schools, and the role that LEAs should play.

NOTES

1 T Brighouse, Article on New Labour's Educational Policies in *Political Quarterly*, forthcoming, 2001

2 Secretaries of State for England and Wales, *Choice and Diversity: a new framework for schools*, Cm 2021, HMSO, 1992

3 Office for Standards in Education, *Access and Achievement in Urban Education*, HMSO, 1993

4 Office for Standards in Education, *The Teaching of Reading in 45 Inner London Primary Schools*, OFSTED, 1996

5 Social Exclusion Unit, *Truancy and School Exclusion*, Cm 3957, 1998

6 Social Exclusion Unit, *Bridging the Gap: new opportunities for 16–18-year-olds not in education, employment or training*, Cm 4405, 1999

7 Social Exclusion Unit, *Bringing Britain Together: a national strategy for neighbourhood renewal*, Cm 4045, 1998

8 Department for Education and Employment, *Skills*, Report of PAT 2, 2000

9 Department for Education and Employment, *Improving the Educational Chances of Children and Young People from Disadvantaged Areas, Schools Plus*, PAT 11, 2000

10 Social Exclusion Unit, *Young People*, SEU Report of PAT 12, 2000

11 See note 2

12 D Blunkett, 'Transforming Secondary Education', speech to the Social Market Foundation, March 2000

13 See House of Commons Select Committee for Education and Employment, *Early Years*, Volume One, The Stationery Office, 2001

14 Audit Commission, *Education Action Zones: meeting the challenge – the lessons identified from the first 25 zones*, The Stationery Office, 2001

15 Department for Education and Employment, 'Education and Training Expenditure since 1990/91', *Statistics Bulletin* 06/00, September 2000

16 See note 1

17 Department for Education and Employment, 'Class Sizes and Pupil Teacher Ratios in England', *Statistics Bulletin* 12/00, December 2000

18 For example, A Heath, 'The Political Arithmetic Tradition in the Sociology of Education', *Oxford Review of Education*, 26(3 and 4), pp313-332

5 Health and poverty

Mary Shaw, Daniel Dorling,
David Gordon and George Davey Smith

WHAT ARE THE ISSUES?

The situation which faced the incoming Labour Government of 1997 was that while many indicators of the population's health – such as life expectancy and infant mortality rates – had been improving steadily throughout the century, inequalities in health had widened significantly during the previous two decades. This widening gap could be seen in both social and geographical terms. For example, research into differences in life expectancy by occupational social class reports that in the period 1992-96 the life expectancy gap between social classes I and V was 9.5 years for men and 6.4 for women; in the period 1972-76 these figures were 5.5 and 5.4 years respectively.[1] In spatial terms, the difference in life chances between areas has been polarising since the early 1980s, and in the most recent period was found to be at the widest ever recorded.[2] These social and spatial health inequalities had been preceded by widening socio-economic inequalities.[3]

A starkly polarised society is the context into which British children are currently being born and raised. This is a society where the life chances of their parents are more unequal than those of their grandparents. Government policies to date can, at best, only have helped to slow down that process. The underlying trend is still one of widening polarisation. As a country we should be aiming, at the very least, for the inequalities in health that will be experienced by our children to be no greater than those experienced by their grandparents. This is not a utopian ideal. The 1950s and 1960s were not a golden age and life expectancy in general was, of course, lower and general health worse. However, improvements in health and increases in life expectancy have not been equally distributed throughout the population.

Figure 1 presents statistics which refer to data up to and including the end of 1998 (the latest available). Here, geographical areas (using old county borough boundaries in order to make comparisons over time) are divided into ten equal-sized groups (or deciles) of areas in terms of population. The standardised mortality ratios (SMR) for deaths under the age of 65 are then calculated for each of these groups.[4] SMRs which are greater than 100 indicate higher chances of mortality, and those less than 100 indicate lower chances of mortality, all relative to the national average.

The figure shows starkly that inequalities in mortality have continued to rise throughout the period 1993 to 1998. In 1990–92 all people living in the decile areas with the highest mortality rates were 42 per cent more likely to die prematurely than the national average. This rose to a rate 50 per cent higher than the national average in the latest time period. Relative mortality ratios also rose for the second, third and fourth deciles (the second, third and fourth highest mortality groups of areas) which illustrates that the polarisation of life chances was not just adversely affecting the most extreme group, but up to 40 per cent of society. At the other extreme, the chances of premature

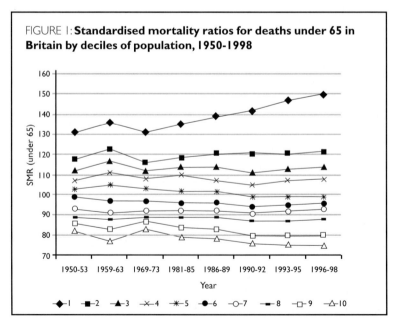

FIGURE 1: **Standardised mortality ratios for deaths under 65 in Britain by deciles of population, 1950-1998**

death among those living in areas with the best life chances declined slightly, from 76 per cent to 75 per cent of the national average.

When comparing the very lowest mortality decile to the highest mortality decile a ratio can be used to illustrate the magnitude of the difference between them. That ratio reached 2.01 by 1998 which means that people under the age of 65 and living in the highest mortality areas of Britain were, by then, *twice* as likely to die in those years as were those under 65 and living in the lowest mortality areas of Britain. Improvements in living standards, and in health and life chances, have thus been enjoyed most by those groups who were already better off and who had relatively better health outcomes to begin with.

Socio-economic inequalities have the effect of producing health inequalities among children, and likewise, health inequalities that can be observed among adults have a knock-on effect on the health of children. If we are to consider the health of children we should focus not only on that age group, but also on the health of families (and especially, of course, women) who are having and bringing up children. Here we present just a small selection of the evidence relating to child health inequalities in Britain.

PREMATURITY, LOW BIRTH WEIGHT AND INFANT MORTALITY

At the very beginning of life there are clear socio-economic differences in the health of babies in Britain. Poverty, poor housing and unemployment all have an effect upon maternal health, which in turn affects foetal health. Babies born to poorer families are more likely to be born prematurely and to be of low birth weight.[5] This has a number of important implications, including a greater likelihood of impaired development, cerebral palsy, and of certain chronic diseases – including coronary heart disease, hypertension and diabetes – in later life.[6] While rates of infant mortality (deaths in the first year of life) continue to fall, babies born to couple parents in manual social classes continue to be at higher risk – death rates for infants whose parents are classified as being in classes IV-V remain between 50 per cent and 65 per cent higher than in classes I-II.[7] In addition, babies of lone mothers – who are particularly likely to live in poverty – also have higher mortality rates.[8] Unfortunately, the Government's 'official' poverty statistics (the *Households Below Average Income* series) assumes that an additional adult will cost a household more than seven babies under two years old.[9] The poverty of families with young children is, therefore, often severely underestimated in official statistics.

ILLNESS AND DISABILITY

Children in poorer families are more likely to experience illness. There is evidence of a socio-economic gradient for the following conditions: infant respiratory infections, childhood respiratory infection, gastro-enteritis, *Helicobacter pylori* infection (an infection acquired in early life which is associated with increased risk of peptic ulcers and stomach cancer in later life), dental caries, tuberculosis and HIV.[10] A study of *Helicobacter pylori* infection in children, for example, found that it was more likely to be found in children from overcrowded homes, in lone-parent families, in rented rather than owned homes and in children attending schools which were classed as having a deprived catchment area.[11] There is also a clear social class gradient for limiting long-term illness (LLTI), as measured in the Census,[12] such that there are 1.4 times as many children with a LLTI in social class V families as would be expected had they had the average rate of illness for all children. Gordon and Heslop have also estimated that 55 per cent of disabled children and their families live in or on the margins of poverty.[13]

INJURY AND ACCIDENTS

Injury and poisoning is now the major category of cause of death for children. Although the overall rates of death from these causes have been falling in the past couple of decades, children whose parents do unskilled manual work are now five times more likely to die from injury or poisoning than are children whose parents have professional occupations.[14] Injury rates are higher among the children of lone mothers,[15] indicative of the link between child injuries and deprivation. Children living in temporary accommodation or poor quality social housing are at greater risk from fire[16] and those living in homes that are not near play areas are at greater risk from pedestrian accidents.[17] Accidents in aggregate are not a matter of fate but, like other forms of morbidity and mortality, are strongly related to factors of social organisation – children from poorer backgrounds are more likely to be injured and to die in road traffic accidents, even though their own parents are less likely to have a car.

Changes in the socio-economic profile of Britain in the past two decades have had a particular impact upon households with children. In the past two decades the proportion of lone-parent households, children in families with no earner and the proportion of households with children living in poverty have all increased.[18] The recent *Poverty and Social Exclusion Survey of Britain* showed that 18 per cent of British children in 1999 were suffering from multiple deprivation, even after the sacrifices made by their parents. These children had to go without two or more necessities such as 'a warm waterproof coat', 'toys and educational games' or 'celebrations on special occasions such as birthdays or Christmas', due to lack of money.[19] These issues are discussed more fully in Chapter 1. It is within this context – of clear evidence of the impact of socio-economic position on the health of children and of socio-economic polarisation directly impacting on the lives of children – that current policy must be appraised. As Reading has said:

> The links between poverty and child health are extensive, strong, and pervasive...virtually all aspects of health are worse among children living in poverty than among children from affluent families.[20]

PROGRESS SINCE 1997

WHAT DOES THE MOST RECENT DATA INDICATE?

In this section we look at the most recent data that we have on the most extreme form of health inequality between different groups of children – their chances of not living beyond childhood. Here we update data presented in *The Widening Gap*,[21] which used 1997 parliamentary constituencies as the geographical unit. In that report the one million people living in the constituencies with the 'best health' were compared with the one million people in the constituencies with the 'worst health'. The indicator of health used to determine the areas of 'best' and 'worst' health was the SMR for deaths under the age of 65, as it is for this group that the greatest scope to narrow the health gap exists. Originally we compared the 'best' and 'worst' health areas for the time period 1991-95; here we revisit those same areas to see how rates have changed in the most recent period of 1996-98. Table 1 lists those original 'worst' and 'best' health areas in terms of their rates of child mortality. (Note that these are the areas where SMRs for all deaths

TABLE 1: **Infant and child mortality rates per 10,000 per year by age in the 'worst' and 'best' health areas of Britain, 1991-95 and 1996-1998**

Name	Rate aged 0		Rate aged 1 to 4		Rate aged 5 to 14		Obs 0 to 14	
	91-95	96-98	91-95	96-98	91-95	96-98	91-95	96-98
Ratio of 'worst health' to 'best health' areas	2.0	1.5	2.0	2.4	1.8	1.6	2.2	1.8
Glasgow Shettleston	109.7	60.8	3.9	3.4	1.5	3.0	57	24
Glasgow Springburn	67.9	119.3	3.4	1.0	2.8	1.3	49	37
Glasgow Maryhill	72.6	66.7	4.1	2.6	2.2	2.5	55	30
Glasgow Pollok	84.9	52.9	2.3	1.6	2.2	2.3	57	24
Glasgow Anniesland	103.0	35.0	4.0	5.9	2.2	2.0	61	20
Glasgow Baillieston	80.4	57.9	6.3	2.9	3.1	2.7	77	32
Manchester Central	88.6	59.1	5.5	2.5	1.8	2.3	111	47
Glasgow Govan	86.1	66.1	7.2	1.0	2.1	2.2	62	25
Liverpool Riverside	62.9	79.6	4.0	2.9	2.9	0.6	68	35
Manchester Blackley	69.9	78.0	4.7	4.6	2.2	1.4	84	50
Greenock and Inverclyde	94.1	65.9	4.1	0	0.5	1.7	44	18
Salford	73.0	52.5	7.2	1.5	2.4	0.6	78	24
Tyne Bridge	106.3	56.6	3.1	2.0	1.4	1.1	89	30
Glasgow Kelvin	54.9	186.3	2.2	3.8	2.0	1.6	20	32
Southwark North and Bermondsey	124.6	84.9	5.6	2.3	1.8	1.2	121	49
'Worst health' million	86.4	70.9	4.7	2.5	2.1	1.7	1033	477

Wokingham	53.2	34.3	2.0	0.7	1.2	1.4	46	19
Woodspring	30.0	51.2	2.0	2.5	0.9	0.6	23	19
Romsey	54.3	49.8	0.5	0	1.1	0.3	33	15
Sheffield Hallam	39.1	37.2	3.9	0	2.0	1.2	28	11
South Cambridgeshire	41.1	55.4	2.7	0.8	2.0	1.4	40	24
Chesham and Amersham	38.2	51.6	2.9	1.6	1.0	0.8	33	22
South Norfolk	35.7	69.0	2.8	1.6	1.4	1.8	33	30
West Chelmsford	42.0	60.7	1.6	0.7	0.5	0.8	36	28
South Suffolk	46.0	32.6	1.6	0	1.1	0	30	8
Witney	39.4	38.4	3.4	2.5	1.3	2.2	44	28
Esher and Walton	51.6	39.1	1.9	0	0.5	1.0	41	20
Northavon	47.9	41.3	2.6	1.2	1.4	1.2	49	25
Buckingham	38.0	48.8	2.9	1.6	1.1	0.9	32	21
'Best health' million	43.2	46.9	2.3	1.0	1.2	1.0	468	270
Britain	63.3	59.0	3.1	1.6	1.6	1.4	34,025	17,578

Source: M Shaw, D Gordon, D Dorling, G Davey Smith, *The Widening Gap: health inequalities and policy in Britain*, Table 2.2, The Policy Press, 1999, and analysis by authors

Key to table:
Rate aged 0   Death rate per 10,000 in first year of life
Rate aged 1 to 4   Death rate per 10,000 for ages 1 to 4 inclusive
Rate aged 5 to 14   Death rate per 10,000 for ages 5 to 14 inclusive
Obs 0 to 14   Total number of deaths of children aged 0 to 14 inclusive

under 65 were highest in 1991-95, not the areas with the highest under-65 SMRs in 1996-98 or the areas with the highest child mortality rates, although there is considerable overlap.)

The results presented in Table 1 should be interpreted with caution, but it can be read to suggest that perhaps the trend is beginning to improve. It is, of course, impossible at this point in time to equate changing trends in child mortality with current government policies. Indeed the latest period we consider (1996-98) was shared between John Major's and Tony Blair's administrations. Nevertheless, using the measure of infant mortality, inequalities between these extreme areas are falling, from a two-fold difference in 1991-95 to being 50 per cent higher in 1996-98. These are the most reliable figures as they are based on the highest number of deaths. There has been a slight worsening of the situation among one to four year-olds – however, the numbers involved are far too small to draw any firm conclusions (indeed, in some constituencies in the period 1996-98 there were no deaths in this age group), whereas for older children inequalities appear to be narrowing.

Looking at individual years of data, the bulk of the improvements recorded above took place in 1998 (results not shown). Future studies will help to show whether this might perhaps be evidence of the first effects of the very modest redistribution which has taken place since 1997. It will take several more years of data and far more sophisticated analysis following cohorts of children to be at all sure. It is certainly too early for interventions such as Sure Start or health action zones to have had an impact, but perhaps the early implementation of policies such as the increase in children's benefits and the improvements in employment trends could be starting to have an effect. At any rate it would be churlish not to point out that in some cases, ever so slightly, things are getting better.

PROGRESS IN TERMS OF POLICY

The New Labour Government has placed the tackling of health inequalities high on its agenda, and is beginning to recognise that while the role of the health service and of health promotion are essential, the key solutions to reducing inequalities lie beyond the realm of health policies. The Government has shown its commitment to tackling health inequalities mostly through the publication of numerous reports, such as Acheson's *Independent Inquiry into Inequalities in Health*[22] and its accompanying Action Report, and *Saving Lives: our healthier nation*.[23] In his report Acheson focussed on the need to begin with policies that improve health in childhood (and even before) as did its precursor of some two decades earlier, the Black Report.[24] There has been a tranche of policy initiatives that will have helped to slow down the trend towards increasing inequalities, but these have often been implemented in order to halt the *growth* of particular levels of material deprivation, rather than to *reverse* current trends.

- Child benefit has been raised from £11.05 to £15.50 (in April 2001) for the first child and changes in the child allowances for income-related benefits have also benefited households with children.
- Working families' tax credit has now been introduced and has had a great effect on improving the standard of living of children who are poor in families where an adult has work.
- The Sure Start programme has been initiated, which although it is sparing in its distribution is at least targeted at the poorest areas. However, there remain many poor children living in affluent areas and they will not be helped by policies that are aimed only at the most deprived areas. They will only be helped by general economic policies of redistribution from rich to poor households.

The above, and many other initiatives which have been implemented or planned by the Government, can be regarded as a good start to tackling inequalities, but there remains much to be done. What has been achieved is certainly a huge improvement on the regressive policies of the last government. However, while an emphasis on getting people into work is undoubtedly beneficial there will always remain a number of adults who are unable to work or who cannot find work – and hence it is vital that strategies aimed at tackling poverty include those who have no prospect of paid work.

TASKS STILL TO BE DONE

The latest evidence presented above should give optimism to policy makers that social conditions and inequalities can change and can change quickly. The current Government has stated that tackling inequalities could take as long as a generation, but the evidence of the rate of change in the past does not support this rather prudent and pessimistic outlook. It has not been the case in the past that change has been slow, it is not the case now and there is no need for it to be the case in the future – if the commitment is really there. What should the Government do now?

Firstly, the Government needs to stop thinking in implicit terms (and sometimes explicitly stating) that there is a group of 'undeserving' poor adults. Employment rates are at a 20-year high. More people are in work in Britain today than ever before. However, in some areas there is little chance that unemployment can be further reduced and many of the new jobs that are being created are very low paid. In an increasing number of cases two parents are both having to work long hours to receive meagre incomes to support their children. Market forces will not help to improve this situation.

Secondly, the world in which children are being brought up is still far more socially divided than was the world of their parents a generation ago. The school they attend and whether they gain access to further or higher education depends very much on the family into which they are born. Despite recent innovation and investment in primary and secondary education, and policies to widen participation in the higher education sector, there are worrying contradictory policies which are serving to increase inequalities in educational outcomes and in access to education. These include school league tables, student loans (rather than grants) and the charging of fees for higher education, as well as indirect factors such as rising house prices in certain areas. However, education is very much in the control of government. It is government which allows educational divides among our children to be maintained and to grow. Government could do far more to avert this. These issues are discussed in more detail in Chapter 4.

Thirdly, there are particular policies that could be adopted to improve the health of children. The Government has increased disability allowances for children, including many with the very worst health – but they and their families remain among the poorest in Britain. The Government should also extend anti-discrimination legislation to cover disabled children and their families. As the children of lone parents are particularly likely to suffer poor health, this group needs particular help, whether they are in work or, for whatever reason, unable to work. While redistributing resources to those who are worst off means that those who are better off will have to make some sacrifices in material terms, it does not mean that the health of the better off will have to suffer. Instead, due to the context of the steady improvements in health we have been seeing, it means that improvements in the health of the better off might slow down, in order for those who have not been enjoying improvements at the same rate to catch up.

Fourthly, the health of young people 'looked after' by local authorities is particularly bad compared with their peers.[25] Specific inter-agency health policies are needed urgently to tackle the problems of these vulnerable children.[26] More also needs to be done for vulnerable teenage children who are homeless. In particular, the Government should restore the right of all 16 and 17-year-olds to social assistance if they need it.

CONCLUSION

The health of children is vital not only in the short term, but also in the long term. Recent research that has taken a life course perspective shows that the social and biological beginnings of life are important for the child's potential for adult health, and that health outcomes in later life are the product of the accumulation of advantage or disadvantage. There is now evidence that a number of conditions have their origins, at least in part, in early life, or accumulate through life.[27] The health of children is thus crucial, now and for the future.

In terms of improving child health, the conclusion of the Black Report still has relevance and resonance today:

> Above all, we consider that the abolition of child poverty should be adopted as a national goal for the 1980s.[28]

We know that child health is related to poverty and inequality, and that any moves towards redistribution will have a beneficial outcome in this regard. A recent study which looked to the future and at the potential of current government policies reported that, at a conservative estimate, the eradication of child poverty would save the lives of 1,400 children under the age of 15 in Britain a year.[29] This should be a powerful incentive to the Government to continue with the aim of eradicating child poverty, in policy and not only in rhetoric, and to do so promptly.

NOTES

1 L Hattersley, 'Trends in Life Expectancy by Social Class: an update', *Health Statistics Quarterly* 2, 1999, pp16-24

2 R Mitchell, D Dorling and M Shaw, *Inequalities in Life and Death: what if Britain were more equal?* A Report for the Joseph Rowntree Foundation, The Policy Press, 2000

3 M Shaw, D Gordon, D Dorling and G Davey Smith, *The Widening Gap: health inequalities and policy in Britain*, The Policy Press, 1999; M Shaw, D Gordon, D Dorling, R Mitchell and G Davey Smith, 'Increasing Mortality Differentials by Residential Area Level of Poverty: Britain 1981-1997', *Social Science and Medicine* 51(1), 2000, pp151-3

4 SMRs, or age-sex-standardised mortality ratios indicate the ratio of the number of deaths observed in the study group or population to the number that would be expected if the study population had the same age-sex-specific rates as the standard population, multiplied by 100. This measure

allows groups with different age distributions to be compared.

5 A MacFarlane and M Mugford, 'Characteristics of Parents and the Circumstances in which they Live', in *Birth Counts: statistics of pregnancy and childbirth*, HMSO, 1984

6 See for example, D Kuh and Y Ben-Shlomo (eds), *A Life Course Approach to Chronic Disease Epidemiology*, Oxford Medical Publications, 1997

7 M Whitehead and F Drever, 'Narrowing Social Inequalities in Health? Analysis of trends in mortality among babies of lone mothers', *British Medical Journal* 318, 1998, p908

8 See note 7

9 The *Households Below Average Income* (HBAI) series takes into account the size and composition of the households in which individuals live. This is based on the assumption that households of different size and composition will require different incomes in order to enjoy a similar standard of living. The process of adjusting income in this way is referred to as equivalisation. In the HBAI equivalence scale the weighting given to a child aged 0-1 is 0.07, whereas the weighting for a head of household is 0.55, more than seven times as much.

10 R Reading, 'Social Disadvantage and Infection in Childhood,' *Sociology of Health and Illness* 19, 1997, pp395-414

11 P Patel, M Mendall, S Khulusi, T C Northfield and D P Strachan, 'Helicobacter Pylori Infection in Childhood: risk factors and effect on growth', *British Medical Journal* 309, 1994, pp1119-23

12 D Gordon and P Heslop, 'Poverty and Disabled Children', in D Dorling and S Simpson (eds), *Statistics in Society: the arithmetic of politics*, Arnold, 1999

13 See note 12

14 I Roberts and C Power, 'Does the Decline in Child Injury Mortality Vary by Social Class? A comparison of class specific mortality in 1981 and 1991', *British Medical Journal* 313, 1996, pp784-6

15 I Roberts and B Pless, 'Social Policy as a Cause of Childhood Accidents: the children of lone mothers, *British Medical Journal* 311, 1995, pp925-8

16 Home Office, *Household Fires in England and Wales: information from the 1994 British Crime Survey*, 1994

17 B A Mueller, F P Rivara, L Shyh-Mine et al, 'Environmental Factors and the Risk for Childhood Pedestrian-Motor Vehicle Collision Occurrence', *American Journal of Epidemiology* 132, 1990, pp550-60

18 See note 3

19 D Gordon, A Adelman, K Ashworth, J Bradshaw, R Levitas, S Middleton, C Pantazis, D Patsios, S Payne, P Townsend and J Williams, *Poverty and Social Exclusion in Britain*, Joseph Rowntree Foundation, 2000

20 R Reading, 'Poverty and the Health of Children and Adolescents', *Archives of Disease in Childhood* 76, 1997, pp463-467

21 See note 3

22 Acheson Report, *Independent Inquiry into Inequalities in Health*, Report of

the Scientific Advisory Group (Chair, Sir Donald Acheson), The Stationery Office, 1998

23 Department of Health, *Saving Lives: our healthier nation*, Cm 4386, The Stationery Office, 1999

24 Department of Health and Social Security, *Inequalities in Health: report of a working group*, 1980

25 See note 22

26 W Utting, *People Like Us: the report of the review of the safeguards for children living away from home*, The Stationery Office, 1997

27 See note 6

28 See note 24, p206

29 See note 2

6 Housing under New Labour

Matthew Waters

The Labour Government was elected with a manifesto that included a number of housing issues, in particular a commitment to strengthen the rights of homeless households, to license parts of the private rented sector with the worst safety conditions – houses in multiple occupation – and to launch major reforms of the welfare benefits system. The manifesto also promised the release of capital receipts from council house sales.

In common with many other policy areas, the new Government appeared to hit the ground running. Within weeks of the election the then Housing Minister, Hilary Armstrong, in her first major speech, announced changes to the recently introduced Housing Act 1996 that would give homeless people better access to social housing. This was the first step in delivering the manifesto commitment to strengthen the safety net for homeless people. Her department also published proposals that would enable councils to spend the capital receipts accumulated from Right to Buy sales of council homes. Also within the first hundred days, the Department of Social Security announced the withdrawal of the previous Government's plans to extend housing benefit 'single room rent' restrictions to single people aged over 25.

After these measures, however, and as with so many other policy areas, the initiatives appeared to be held up by the Government's Comprehensive Spending Review. Until this was finalised, the previous government's budgets remained. No new money was available and any new initiatives had to be funded from within current expenditure. Capital receipts were the only significant exception to this edict. The spending reviews were important for housing, but more significant in terms of mapping the Government's future housing policies was the publication of the housing Green Paper in April 2000. Many of the measures in the Green Paper will only come to fruition in a possible second term. It appears that this is when the Government hopes to deliver on housing. Delivering better and more affordable housing must be a key plank in achieving the Government's objective of eliminating child poverty in a generation.

EXPENDITURE ON HOUSING

The first two years of the Government's spending programme on housing merely matched the previous administration's expenditure plans – and these plans included a decrease in real terms. The Comprehensive Spending Review of 1998 held that year's expenditure and increased it by inflation the following year.

A clear picture of the impact of this decline in spending can be gleaned from the new social house building statistics. Only approximately 20,000 new social rented homes were built in 1999, half the number achieved by the previous government in 1995.

The total expenditure on social housing has been boosted by the capital receipts money being released to local councils – a total of around £5 billion in five years – although much of this money has gone to improving the state of the council stock rather than building new socially rented homes. However, the reduction and finally the ending of mortgage interest relief for homeowners reduces significantly the Government's overall expenditure on housing.

The Comprehensive Spending Review of July 2000 is, however, perhaps the acid test. In this year's review social housing was a winner, with the announcement of increased expenditure year on year until 2003/04, nearly doubling expenditure inside three years.

When matched against housing need, it is clear that the Government still has a lot more to do. Shelter estimates 100,000 new social homes are required each year to meet both current and rising housing need. The Government's programme falls far short of this target, both now and even with the budgeted increases for a second term.

HOMELESSNESS AND SOCIAL EXCLUSION

The above mentioned change in homelessness legislation was announced soon after the election. It was a welcome move, but it was not until 2000 that the Government's overall direction for housing became clear.

While the number of households accepted as homeless has increased only slightly during the lifetime of the Government, the number of homeless households living in temporary accommodation has increased significantly, for the first time passing 71,000 households in September 2000.[1] It is clear that the lack of move-on accommodation is a significant factor.

Even more worryingly, the number of households living in bed and breakfast accommodation has reached record levels. In September 2000, 9,530 households were being housed in bed and breakfasts by local authorities, a rise of 14 per cent on the previous year.[2] The use of such accommodation shows no sign of reducing significantly. The impact of living in bed and breakfasts is particularly hard on families with children, and the health risks in this sort of accommodation, in particular the risk of some infections and of accidents, are high.

The setting up of the Rough Sleepers Unit and the appointment of a homelessness 'czar' were significant moves and have shown the Government's resolve to end this specific manifestation of social exclusion. The adoption of the target to reduce the numbers of people sleeping on the streets by two-thirds within three years is undoubtedly bold. These numbers have begun to be reduced, with those who have been there the longest being targeted for help first. The success of this strategy will rely on there being an adequate number of both hostel and move-on beds and the availability of specialist advice and assistance services, including drug and alcohol counselling.

A controversial part of the rough sleeping strategy has been the use of adverts encouraging people not to give to people begging on the streets but instead to donate to a government-sponsored collection. This will then be distributed to a range of charities offering practical help and support for street sleepers. This has not been supported by all organisations working with homeless people. Nevertheless, it is to be hoped that the overall rough sleeping strategy does succeed in offering a real alternative to life on the streets, with support and long-term accommodation.

HOUSING BENEFIT

The Government's plans to reform and update the welfare system have undoubtedly been ambitious. Perhaps the key to long-term success, however, is to reform the benefit arguably most in need of major change, and yet conversely the most difficult to reform – housing benefit.The welfare reform Green Paper was issued in 1998. Expected to set a radical agenda, not least on housing benefit, it proposed instead limited measures.

To many, housing benefit is in crisis.Administration is painfully slow in too many areas, with tenants facing the risk of eviction due to the failure to administer and pay benefit within reasonable timescales. Many face shortfalls between their rent and the housing benefit payable, even though cheaper accommodation may not be available. The hardship caused has been dramatic for some, with shortfalls of £40 per week or more.The impact on poverty of these restrictions and the consequent threat of rent arrears and possible eviction cannot be overstated. Meanwhile, the introduction of tax credits highlights how far the Government has come in proposing new ways of delivering welfare benefits to those in work. However, the interaction with housing benefit has reduced the impact of tax credits for those in rented housing, as increased income from credits is often eroded by reduced help with rent.

The Government has focused heavily on the issue of fraud and its prevention. However, the introduction of various measures, including the verification framework, has been blamed, in part at least, for increased administration problems and delays.

A critical report by the Social Security Select Committee was published in July and highlighted many of the problems.[3] It called on the Government to adopt a range of policies for solving the crisis.The Government's response to the report[4] was disappointing and proposed few clear initiatives for solving the problems with housing benefit administration.

THE HOUSING GREEN PAPER

Announced in the Budget of March 1999, the housing Green Paper[5] was due to be published in the autumn of that year. When finally published, nearly six months late, it was a very different document from that originally envisaged. The Budget statement suggested a Green

Paper covering housing benefit and increased choice in social housing lettings. When it finally appeared it covered a much greater range of housing issues and offered possibly the most comprehensive review of housing policy for a generation. The title of the Green Paper, *Quality and Choice: a decent home for all*, was particularly welcome, recognising that achieving this should be the aim of government policy.

The Green Paper floated many ideas and not all will see the light of day. It presented a much clearer sense of the Government's direction and focus. It reviewed homelessness policy and practice and concluded that changes were needed. New groups are likely to be given rights under homelessness legislation, in particular 16 and 17-year-olds, people fleeing violence in the home and people from institutionalised backgrounds.

Introducing licensing for people living in houses in multiple occupation was reiterated in the housing Green Paper. A manifesto commitment, this will also require parliamentary time to implement and it looks as if this will have to wait until a possible second term. Certainly the implementation of any statutory licensing scheme will have to wait, even if parliamentary time is found now to introduce the legislation.

Rents for most local authority tenants are significantly lower than for tenants of registered social landlords (RSLs), although it is the variation in rents within each of these sectors that creates confusion and incoherence. The Green Paper announced the intention to create a clearer social housing rents structure, with greater equalisation. It will be a painful time for many RSLs and maybe even for local authority tenants, but rationalising rents in the social housing sector is long overdue. Again, although moves are being made now, this is a long-term project.

Another measure included in the Green Paper was the continuation and enhancement of the transfer of local authority housing stocks, whereby RSLs can take over the ownership and management of council estates and provide increased investment. The possibility that local authorities could also set up 'arms length' companies to continue managing their stock was also put forward. Who owns social housing looks set to continue to be a major debate in the next Parliament.

Housing benefit provided perhaps the most disappointing aspect of the Green Paper. For a document supposedly designed to update housing benefit policy and administration, it was woefully thin on real initiatives to improve this benefit. The problems were recognised and highlighted, but the solutions did not appear to be comprehensive.

Longer-term reform options – either paying housing benefit as a 'flat rate' benefit or providing an incentive for tenants to 'shop around' for cheaper accommodation – appear to have been put off until social housing rents are reformed. Flat rates concern many because of their possible impact of creating even greater shortfalls between the rent charged and the help available through welfare benefits. This may, however, be an issue for a second term as it becomes increasingly clear that housing benefit continues to be a block to tenants feeling the full benefits of other welfare reforms, including meeting poverty targets.

THE FUTURE

The Government has had a large agenda to put into action – a series of reforms laying the foundations for change. As such, it is not surprising that there is much that still needs to be done to improve housing.

The money announced in the Comprehensive Spending Review 2000 is a big step in the right direction. But it is only if the Government were to win a second term that the programme to greatly increase social house building would be delivered.

Two significant manifesto commitments remain outstanding – increasing protection for homeless people and licensing the worst parts of the private rented sector. If these are not delivered during this Parliament, the Government will be seen to have failed to meet its commitments on housing.

On protection for homeless people, the publication of the Homes Bill in December 2000, following the Green Paper consultation, will lead to new requirements for local authorities to develop strategies to prevent homelessness in their areas. It will also give homeless households greater rights to secure long-term accommodation and increase choice in lettings policies. In addition, it will update the home-buying process, with new requirements for sellers to provide information to prospective buyers. It is likely these provisions will be implemented only if the Government secures a second parliamentary term. Regulations are nevertheless expected to be laid before Parliament to increase the homeless groups who should be accepted as in priority need for social housing.

Licensing of limited sections of the private rented sector, however, does not appear to feature in the current parliamentary session. It is unlikely, therefore, that this measure will be enacted in the lifetime of this Parliament. At least one manifesto commitment will not have been met. The challenge will be to ensure it remains a part of any new manifesto commitment.

Meanwhile, housing benefit administration is still in crisis. Either simplification will need to be brought forward or more radical reform will have to be undertaken sooner than expected.

A recent statement detailing government initiatives following the responses to the Green Paper appears to show a change in attitude towards housing benefit.[6] There is a clearer recognition of the administrative crisis in many areas, and a commitment to provide the help and resources required to overcome this. It is to be hoped this signals a change in the Government's approach to housing benefit and a new commitment to ensure it provides the support and help required by tenants on the lowest incomes. The Green Paper itself did not offer much comfort for those tenants facing significant shortfalls between their rent and the amount of housing benefit paid, and this most recent statement did little to suggest this area would be reviewed and tackled, at least not in the short term.

The response to the Green Paper consultation also flags up the position in the devolved administrations, where parallel measures to those discussed above are at various stages of development within the specific contexts of Scotland, Wales and Northern Ireland.[7]

Social housing has a crucial part to play in promoting social inclusion and in meeting many of the Government's other agendas, including a major role in meeting the objective to end child poverty in 20 years. There will be an expectation that this will begin to be delivered during any second term in power.

NOTES

1 Department of the Environment, Transport and the Regions, *Statutory Homelessness Statistics: third quarter 2000*, 2000
2 Department of the Environment, Transport and the Regions, 2000
3 *Sixth Report: Housing Benefit*, HC 385-1, 2000
4 Department of Social Security, *Report on Housing Benefit,* Cm 4869, 2000
5 Department of the Environment, Transport and the Regions/Department of Social Security, *Quality and Choice: a decent home for all – the way forward for housing*, 2000
6 Department of the Environment, Transport and the Regions/Department of Social Security, *Quality and Choice: a decent home for all – the way forward for housing*, 2000
7 See note 6, Introduction, paras 11–14

7
Neighbourhood renewal
Pete Alcock

SPATIAL INEQUALITY

Over the last decade or so, concern with spatial inequalities has come to occupy an increasingly important place in more general academic and political debate about the problem of poverty. A significant sign of this was CPAG's own publication on the social geography of poverty,[1] which provided graphic evidence of the variation in the extent and depth of poverty and deprivation across the UK. More recently the Department of the Environment, Transport and the Regions has commissioned a major review of indices of local deprivation, culminating in the publication of a new *Index of Multiple Deprivation*, which measures deprivation down to ward level across six domains (income, employment, health, education, housing and service access) and reveals continuing stark differences between poorer and more affluent areas.[2] There are broad trends here – notably the North-South divide – but at district and neighbourhood (ward) level inequalities are even more pronounced, with the poorest wards having average deprivation scores over ten times those of the most affluent. The new Index also includes a supplementary Child Poverty Index, mapping the extent of dependency upon means-tested benefits of families with children. Here the contrasts are even starker, with the highest ranking wards recording over 75 per cent of families in the area dependent upon means-tested benefits compared with under 7 per cent in the better-off areas.

The research evidence exists, therefore; and it has been taken up in anti-poverty policy planning. In the 1980s Margaret Thatcher was famously photographed on a derelict industrial site in Teesside promising to bring renewed prosperity to Britain's run-down urban areas. The policy response of the time, however, was the urban development corporations (UDCs), which utilised central government resources to promote private property-driven economic revival in a small number of cities – most notably in East London, where the London Docklands Development Corporation spent millions on high profile office space (such as Canary Wharf) but did little to alter the circumstances of the poor people of Tower Hamlets.

After the 1997 general election, New Labour acted swiftly to set a rather different tone for its response to local poverty. In December of that year the Prime Minister announced the establishment of a new Social Exclusion Unit (SEU), responsible directly to the Cabinet Office in No.10, to lead the Government's policies for combating local deprivation. Within a year the SEU had produced a *National Strategy for Neighbourhood Renewal*;[3] and it was clear that within this was a concern to promote social, as well as economic, development at the local level and to focus this in particular on the newly-recognised problem of social exclusion.

LESSONS FROM HISTORY

Local action to combat poverty and deprivation is not a new policy idea, however. In the 1960s the Wilson Government was also concerned with 'pockets of poverty' and had experimented with education priority areas (EPAs), community development projects (CDPs) and urban aid – strong similarities here to the education action zones, the New Deal for communities and Single Regeneration Budget (SRB) currently operating. And these initiatives themselves were closely modelled on anti-poverty programmes developed earlier in the US as part of a federal 'war on poverty', such as Headstart (targeted support for pre-school children, like Labour's Sure Start) and community action projects (similar to the current New Deal for communities).[4] The focus on child poverty, through Headstart and (now) Sure Start was also a significant feature of these local action programmes.

There is nothing wrong with policy transfer over time or across nations, of course; but, if wheels (especially broken ones) are not to be re-invented here, it is important to learn from the lessons of past neighbourhood initiatives. And here the messages are rather mixed. The

US 'war on poverty' was abandoned at the end of the 1960s, although there was widespread recognition that it had done little to combat the problems of urban poverty across the country.[5] A similar fate befell the UK's EPAs and CDPs. And here the CDPs in particular were, to a large extent, the (articulate) authors of their own demise, arguing in one of their many publications that expecting small community projects to reverse the trends of economic and social decline experienced in most deprived industrial neighbourhoods amounted to little more than *Gilding the Ghetto*.[6]

The past protagonists of local anti-poverty action discovered that there were inherent limitations to the scope of neighbourhood renewal. However, they also developed a range of initiatives which improved immensely the lives of many poor people. Tenants' organisations, community centres and welfare rights advice and advocacy did much to challenge individual problems of deprivation and exclusion – and most of these initiatives have continued long after the initial programmes which had supported them had gone. In the 1980s and early 1990s the problem of poverty as a focus for national policy concern was dismissed by government and neighbourhood renewal was redirected towards the property development of the UDCs. However, many of the local initiatives begun by previous programmes were not lost, for, as central government moved out, local and supranational government moved in. Many local authorities up and down the country began to develop their own local anti-poverty strategies, taking forward much of the work of previous national programmes[7] and openly challenging national complacency. At the same time the European Union (EU) funded three programmes to combat poverty and social exclusion, which supported a small number of pilot anti-poverty projects in member nations.[8]

One of the important messages for a new Labour government committed to recapturing a concern with neighbourhood deprivation and decline should have been the need to re-connect with the local authority and EU experiences of sustaining local anti-poverty action. However, there is little evidence that the incoming administration did make the re-appraisal of recent experiences of local anti-poverty work a central feature of its policy planning framework.

NEW LABOUR POLICIES

Nevertheless, Labour did act quickly to resurrect concern with the 'p' word. Poverty has been put back on the social agenda, although it has been extended more broadly to embrace the concept of social exclusion. This reaches beyond cash inequalities to include more general problems of physical isolation, denial of services, insecurity and fear; and combating exclusion ties in with a range of other new policy priorities – employment, networks, social capital and citizenship.

Particularly significant in this context, therefore, was the establishment of the SEU. The Unit was described as 'improving understanding ... promoting solutions, encouraging co-operation [and] disseminating best practice.'[9] Furthermore, it was a central example of the Prime Minister's concern to promote 'joined-up solutions to joined-up problems'. It comprised representatives from all the major government departments and had a limited budget – being required to redirect existing resources rather than dish out new ones. The work of the Unit was endorsed by the Green Paper on welfare reform in 1998 which stated that 'there should be specific action to attack social exclusion and help those in poverty'.[10]

One of the early priorities of the SEU was spatial inequality – initially pejoratively described as the country's 'problem estates'. This led in 1998 to its proposals for a national strategy for neighbourhood renewal,[11] from which flowed the New Deal for communities. This was backed by £800 million of new resources to support local community action, initially in 17 'pathfinder' areas, extended later to another 22. The 1998 paper also proposed the establishment of 18 policy action teams (PATs) pulling together ministers, civil servants and external experts to explore policy options across a range of issues associated with social exclusion, such as community self-help and access to financial services. The recommendations from the PATs were part of a consultation on and review of the neighbourhood renewal strategy,[12] with a new policy statement promised for Autumn 2000, alongside White Papers on rural and urban strategies.

The SEU has played a key role in Labour's commitment to neighbourhood renewal, but it is far from acting in isolation. There has been something of an explosion of other area-based policy initiatives, all seeking to challenge different aspects of local poverty and deprivation:

- Sure Start: £540 million for targeted pre-school activities;
- 15 employment zones: to tackle long-term unemployment;
- 26 health action zones: to promote partnership responses to poor health;
- 73 education action zones; to improve performance in poor schools;
- Phoenix Fund: to support small businesses in deprived areas;
- community safety: to promote crime prevention and reduction.

There are also further commitments to an £800 million Neighbourhood Renewal Fund and the setting up of a National Centre for Neighbourhood Renewal. In addition to these new ideas has been the continuation of the SRB. This was established under the Major governments to co-ordinate support for local regeneration partnership activity and to engineer a shift away from the property focus of 1980s urban renewal. Labour has continued to support successive annual rounds of SRB funding for local social and economic regeneration partnership initiatives, selected through a bidding process managed by the regional development agencies. There are now over 890 local schemes which will receive a total of £5.6 billion over seven years, some focused on particular neighbourhoods and others tackling broader issues across local authority districts.

Much has been developed by New Labour, therefore, to target anti-poverty action onto local neighbourhoods. These were discussed in a chapter on communities in the Government's first annual report on poverty and social exclusion, *Opportunity for All*.[13] One of the purposes of this report was to establish indicators against which government policies could be assessed, but it contained no indicators at a local level. The notion of an annual review of indicators had also been promoted in research by the New Policy Institute.[14] They included indicators on community poverty in their list of 50; and in its second report the Government responded to this challenge by setting, as a first step, the following three new indicators to monitor progress at community level:[15]

- a reduction in the disparity in employment rates in the most deprived authorities;
- a reduction in the disparity in domestic burglary rates;
- a reduction in the number of families in homes below decency standards.

The second report also stresses the importance of improving the co-ordination of the plethora of neighbourhood-based programmes now operation in local areas, a point stressed by the Performance and Innovation Unit in February 2000.[16]

EVALUATING ACHIEVEMENTS

The important question, of course, is not how much has been developed to combat local poverty and social exclusion, but how much is being achieved – and indicators of activity are only one part of a more general process of monitoring and evaluation. On the face of it, the Government does seem to be committed to evaluation of anti-poverty activity, with independent research built into most of the neighbourhood renewal programmes, including Sure Start, the action zones and SRB. There is a commitment to learn and the Government has trumpeted its concern that policies should be based on 'what works'; but this is tempered by a concern also to see results. And there is a major contradiction here at the heart of Labour's neighbourhood renewal strategy.

Evaluation takes time. This is especially the case when the process of social change itself is long term; and, where local initiatives are seeking to reverse decades of social and economic deprivation and decline, this is inevitably going to be so. It is too early to expect results from the evaluation of the Government's area-based action programmes; and it is too early to expect major changes to have taken place within those areas where they are focused. Yet the Government, increasingly under pressure from an impending general election, naturally wants early 'hits'. This contradiction cannot be resolved and is likely to lead to frustrations on both sides of the process of policy development and delivery.

However, it is not the only tension underlying the local action strategy. Much has been made in the policy documents underpinning the various area-based programmes of the importance of partnership and participation, of the need for community development and capacity building, of the importance of *bottom-up* as well as *top-down* policy planning. This is an understandable, and laudable, goal. However, it must be set against a programme structure that is determined, and largely managed, by the state (both central and local). Local people and local agencies are invited to join partnership boards and other bodies, but this is not the same thing as community action. Many people living in Britain's poorest neighbourhoods do not have much of a history of collaboration with, or trust in, government agencies; and in many cases this experience is a mutual one. It will take time, and a different process of policy development, to turn this distrust around – and yet time for alternative strategies is not what the Government feels currently to have much of in store.

There are some other, more deep-seated, tensions also lying just beneath the surface of the area-based anti-poverty approach. For a start, although many poor people do live in deprived neighbourhoods, most do not; and those that do not will not benefit from area-based initiatives, even though their exclusion may in some ways be more difficult to bear – for instance, the only recently recognised rural poor. What is more, area initiatives must draw boundary lines around their chosen neighbourhoods. This is as much a political as a policy process, sometimes now dubbed 'postcode politics', where the arguments about the criteria and procedures for selecting the focus for area initiatives become an inevitable source of local (and national) conflict. Success in achieving 'problem area' status can itself be a double-edged sword. Being identified as a deprived neighbourhood can attract an element of 'negative labelling' – both for residents (who may feel themselves to be struggling hard to avoid deprivation) and for external agencies (who may see in the label a confirmation of the lack of confidence in the economic and social potential of the area).

However, the most contentious aspect of the area-based response to poverty and social exclusion is the insidious danger of *pathologisation* which it inevitably carries with it. This is the, sometimes unstated, assumption that, because local people are the victims of social exclusion, they must also be its authors. On the face of it few in government would subscribe to such a bald victimisation of the poor; but the practical effect of the assumption is a subtler one. Local initiatives work with local people to develop local solutions to their problems. This sounds positive, and yet implicit within it is a view that other (more powerful) actors outside need take no action over problems that are not really theirs. To put this into other words, area-based renewal strategies assume that the solution to local problems of poverty and social exclusion lie locally – they do not. This was recognised by the CDP authors in their 1977 report. It was also the conclusion reached by those evaluating the US anti-poverty programmes of the 1960s:

> Serious and considered analysis led to the inescapable conclusion that... deprivation in many areas may not be responsive to programmes of amelioration and community action. The problems of poverty cannot be resolved as if they were isolated from the wider economic, social and political patterns of the nation.[17]

FUTURE ACTION

It is important that local indicators have been included in the Government's second poverty report, therefore, for local targets must be seen to be a part of a broader national strategy if they are to have any realistic hope of transforming the social and economic circumstances of poor people in deprived neighbourhoods – rather than merely ameliorating local problems. This is not to suggest, however, that local action should be abandoned. Just as in the 1960s and 1970s, much is being, and can be, achieved through neighbourhood renewal work – especially where policy intervention recognises the need to challenge paternalism and pathologisation, and promote partnership and participation. This takes time and it requires a commitment to building up the capacity of all potential partners to participate. It requires also the development of policy initiatives that work with local people, rather than impose political preferences and professional judgements on them. As CPAG's 1999 publication argued, people living in poverty should be allowed to 'speak for themselves'.[18]

The important implication of this is that evaluation of policy action must pay as much attention to *process* as it does to *outcome*. Government should be concerned not only with 'what works', but also how it works; and accompanying this is a need to temper expectations of early 'hits'. There is another important message in the second poverty report, however, albeit rather an implicit one. The chapter on communities is here entitled 'Narrowing the Gap'.[19] This suggests a focus upon reducing inequalities as well as combating poverty, which is certainly to be welcomed.

Social inclusion can be promoted by local action, therefore, but this must be placed within the wider context of social exclusion and social polarisation. Inclusion is a broad and all-encompassing policy goal. It requires national economic action to reduce gross inequalities and political debate to promote individual *and* collective responsibility and mutual protection. Changes need to take place outside of the 'problem estates' in order for changes to take place within them; and the suggestion in the autumn of 2000 that the Government may be considering the establishment of a separate Department for Social Inclusion to co-ordinate and spearhead this activity after the general election may give local action just the national profile that it needs to ensure that the latest round of anti-poverty programmes do not provide just another layer of gilt on the ghettos.

NOTES

1 C Philo (ed), *Off the Map: the social geography of poverty in the UK,* CPAG, 1995
2 Department of the Environment, Transport and the Regions, *Indices of Deprivation,* The Stationery Office, 2000
3 Social Exclusion Unit, *Bringing Britain Together: a national strategy for neighbourhood renewal,* Cm 4045, The Stationery Office, 1998
4 J Higgins, *The Poverty Business: Britain and America,* Basil Blackwell and Martin Robertson, 1978
5 E James, *America against Poverty,* Routledge and Kegan Paul, 1970
6 Community Development Project, *Gilding the Ghetto: the state and the poverty experiments,* 1977
7 P Alcock, G Craig, K Dalgliesh and S Pearson, *Combating Local Poverty: the management of anti-poverty strategies by local government,* Local Government Management Board, 1995
8 G Room et al, *Anti-Poverty Action Research in Europe,* School of Advanced Urban Studies, University of Bristol, 1993
9 Social Exclusion Unit's website, www.cabinet-office.gov.uk/seu, 1997
10 Department of Social Security, *New Ambitions for our Country: a new contract for welfare,* Green Paper, Cm 3805, p63, The Stationery Office, 1998
11 See note 3
12 Social Exclusion Unit, *National Strategy for Neighbourhood Renewal: a framework for consultation,* The Stationery Office, 2000; Social Exclusion Unit, *National Strategy for Neighbourhood Renewal, Policy Action Team Report Summaries: a compendium,* The Stationery Office, 2000
13 Department of Social Security, *Opportunity for All: tackling poverty and social exclusion,* First Annual Report, Cm 4445, The Stationery Office, 1999
14 C Howarth, P Kenway, G Palmer and C Street, *Monitoring Poverty and Social Exclusion: Labour's inheritance,* Joseph Rowntree Foundation, 1998 and 1999
15 Department of Social Security, *Opportunity for All, One Year On: making a difference,* Second Annual Report, Cm 4865, The Stationery Office, 2000
16 See note 15
17 K Clark and J Hopkins, *A Relevant War Against Poverty: a study of community action programs and observable social change,* p256, Harper and Row, 1968
18 P Beresford, D Green, R Lister and K Woodard, *Poverty First Hand: poor people speak for themselves,* CPAG, 1999
19 See note 15

8 Race and New Labour

Gary Craig

Evaluating a government's performance in most policy areas is difficult enough. Analysing the performance of a government in terms of a complex and contested area such as 'race' is a considerably less easy task, one made substantially more difficult by the continuing lack of adequate data about the social and economic circumstances of the UK's black and minority ethnic population, a lack which the 1997 Government has largely failed to address. This widespread statistical 'colour-blindness' means that detailed quantitative analyses of poverty and exclusion of children or adults have little – and often no – content based on the dimension of 'race' or ethnicity.[1] Failure of research methodology,[2] particularly the unwillingness or inability of researchers to incorporate an effective 'race' dimension into sample surveys or qualitative investigations, is often a contributing factor to our lack of understanding.

Much of our knowledge of the difficulties faced by Britain's minority groups is thus derived from small-scale qualitative analyses and has frequently been dismissed in the past by governments as unrepresentative. The 2001 Census, with its longer and more sensitive list of ethnic categories and its more explicit recognition of 'hidden' minorities, such as the Irish community in the UK, will provide a better statistical picture than hitherto. However, the limitations of the Census, particularly its ten-year cycle, means that its usefulness as a tool to monitor trends is very limited.

The alternative, of effective ethnic monitoring undertaken by all major public, private and not-for-profit agencies, has yet to be put in place, despite some isolated examples of good practice, although, as noted below, new legislation may change this picture significantly in the life of a future government. Because of limitations of space, this review will not attempt to analyse the performance of all government initiatives in the field of 'race' but will assess the work of the Government's major initiatives in addressing poverty and exclusion. This is appropriate since the continuing marginalisation of members of many minorities – reflected in increased levels of poverty, unemployment, debt, low pay, poor housing and ill-health – is now more extensively highlighted by independent research.[3] In any case, this exploration, in particular through an examination of the work of the Social Exclusion Unit, raises a range of issues across the whole of government. The reader should, however, be reminded that there are many policy issues which cannot be treated in detail here – for example, labour market issues such as the low level at which the minimum wage is currently set, the effectiveness of the New Deal and the new Connexions strategy – which are of particular salience for minority ethnic communities because of their over-representation in poorly-trained, low-paid and marginal work and the failure of these schemes effectively to target minority groups.

THE WORK OF THE SOCIAL EXCLUSION UNIT

The New Labour Government created the Social Exclusion Unit (SEU) in the winter of 1997. In the Government's view social exclusion was 'a shorthand term for what can happen when people or areas suffer from a combination of linked problems, such as unemployment, poor skills, low incomes, poor housing, high crime environments, bad health and family breakdown.' The Unit's remit, discussed in more detail elsewhere in this book, was to provide 'joined-up solutions to joined-up problems'. I have argued elsewhere[4] that the concept of social exclusion raises as many questions about the goals of government as it answers. Nevertheless, and given what research had already told us about the social and economic circumstances of Britain's minority ethnic population,[5] it seemed reasonable to assume that the SEU would regard minority ethnic communities as an important target for its developing work programme. However, questioned in July 1998 at the annual conference of the Social Policy Association about the programme of the SEU and the apparent exclusion of the dimension of 'race' from this work, the (then) Director of the Unit, Moira Wallace, stated to the general dismay of the audience that 'race is not a priority for the SEU'. This stance has clearly been modified in the light of later experience (see below).

Towards the end of the life of this government, however, there have been signs that this position has changed. It is likely that this shift has been occasioned most of all by the findings of the Stephen Lawrence Inquiry[6] (established in July 1997 prior to the creation of the SEU) which appeared in February 1999, leading to a robust nation-wide debate into the nature of institutional racism. While the recommendations of that Inquiry dealt most of all, quite naturally, with the need for change within the police services and associated elements of the criminal justice system, some of its ramifications spilled over into more general questions of the provision of social and welfare services. For example, local education authorities and school governors were urged to develop anti-racist strategies, as were local government and other bodies, founded on an appreciation of cultural diversity, and informing community safety and crime and disorder partnership working.

Clearly the Macpherson Inquiry messages could not, for a government claiming to be concerned with 'joined-up solutions to joined-up problems', be ignored in the context of other policy and service development. Although the discussion below shows that, at best, the response of government might be regarded as uneven, there are now some indications that none of the institutions of welfare will be free, in principle at least, from subjecting their policies and services to an anti-racist perspective. The leverage for this will be provided most of all by the Race Relations (Amendment) Act 2000, itself a direct legacy of the murder of Stephen Lawrence, which will require all public authorities to examine their own work from the perspective of equality of opportunity; that is, to ensure that policy and service development explicitly addresses the issue of 'race' and ethnicity, including by the setting of employment targets. This should help to confront the 'colour-blind' approach of many organisations, including government departments, illustrated by the Department of Social Security's approach to 'tackling poverty and social exclusion'. Its key framework document on indicators of success[7] followed on the publication of *Opportunity for All*. The former sets a range of general targets but only one, the very general 'increase in employment rates of disadvantaged groups...[including] ethnic minorities...' specifically identifies the dimension of 'race'. The history of equal opportunity measures demonstrates strongly that 'colour-blind' approaches to dealing with structural racism will fail on their own; yet most government departments have persisted with them.

Despite the Government's rather dismal start in this field, a few initiatives have been taken which show some willingness to incorporate a 'race' dimension into public policy. For example, in February 2000, the Department of the Environment, Transport and the Regions (belatedly) issued a press notice describing its 'blueprint for ensuring race equality is at the heart of the flagship regeneration programme, the New Deal for communities'.[8] The New Deal for communities (NDC) had itself been launched 18 months earlier and, apart from a very brief aside about the need for 'initiatives which benefit disadvantaged ethnic minorities',[9] there is no perspective on 'race' in the document whatsoever, although the SEU's scoping document[10] provided some background data on the concentration of minority ethnic communities within the neighbourhoods identified as deprived. The 'race' equality guidance raises important issues about process, such as how 'people from black and ethnic minority backgrounds [could be involved] in the NDC process' and 'how to assess the needs of black and ethnic minority communities and monitor whether the programme is meeting those needs', implying that most organisations engaged in the New Deal for communities had some way to go to achieve these tasks. Particularly given the urgency with which other work such as that of the policy action teams (see below) had to be carried through, it is not, however, unreasonable to ask why it took so long for the issue of 'race' equality to find its way into what the Government clearly regards as its major intervention to address the difficulties facing the hundreds of deprived neighbour-hoods within the UK. Seemingly, 'race' was indeed not, until quite belatedly, a government priority.

Further impetus for discussion of the 'race' dimension of public and social policy was also undoubtedly provided by the findings of some of the SEU's early reports. For example, the report on truancy and school exclusion[11] demonstrated that certain minority ethnic groups (particularly those children of African-Caribbean origin) were disproportion-ately represented amongst those truanting and/or excluded from school.

Similarly, the report on 'disaffected' 16–18-year-olds[12] observed that young people 'of African-Caribbean, Pakistani and Bangladeshi origin experience longer periods out of learning and work than their white counterparts'. However, while these and other reports note that contributing factors to this accumulation of difficulties include poverty, disadvantage and disaffection, the structural causes of disaffec-tion are not explored. For example, despite the fact that it is now incontrovertible that Pakistani and Bangladeshi households are more likely to be in poverty than for the population at large,[13] the continuing refusal of the Benefits Agency to consider monitoring the ethnicity of claimants – another example of an institutional 'colour-blindness' – means that the aim of ensuring that its resources are specifically directed towards members of minority ethnic communities in poverty is fundamentally undermined.

The SEU's scoping document referred to above, more hopefully, did report on the establishment of 18 cross-cutting teams (later to be known as policy action teams – PATs), each of which was given the task of addressing specific social or economic issues and was required to report on 'race and ethnic minority issues relevant to their topic'. These PATs reported through 1999 and provided a very full agenda for policy development over the next years. Most PATs give issues of 'race' a fairly cursory treatment, with some even less full in their treatment of it than others. For example, PAT 12,[14] which reported on young people, addressed the question of 'is there an ethnic minority effect' in two paragraphs; this acknowledged that young people from some minority ethnic groups were more at risk of poverty and disengagement, partly as a result of racism and discrimination, but did not develop this specific analysis any further. The PAT 16 report, *Learning Lessons*,[15] contains two recommendations which mention black and minority ethnic communities, one to skew the provision of bursaries for training in management and business skills towards members of minorities, the other to encourage interchange between civil servants and members of minority organisations. Neither of these recommendations is supported by any detailed analysis of the experience of black and minority ethnic organisations and one is left with the impression that these emphases are almost afterthoughts, perhaps hardly surprising given that only one of the 56 organisations consulted by the team was explicitly a black-led organisation.

The report of PAT 9, on community self-help,[16] reporting to Paul Boateng, Junior Home Office Minister, acknowledges, this time in three paragraphs, both the important role of minority ethnic voluntary sector organisations and some of the structural problems of racism which they face: lack of sustained funding, lack of recognition, lack of understanding and an insensitive appreciation of their diversity. This leads on to a recognition of the marginalisation of black and minority ethnic voluntary and community organisations by existing funding mechanisms from both central and local government and the need for funders to provide 'dedicated funding to support local and regional, as well as national infrastructure'. Characteristically, in this context, the working party on central government-voluntary sector relations, charged with developing both a national compact between these parties and codes of guidance,[17] has found the development of a code of guidance for government relations with black and minority ethnic organisations problematic and it will be one of the last to appear. The same pattern has been repeated at a local level in the development of local compacts or in engagement with regeneration initiatives, where, as research also shows,[18] black and minority ethnic organisations continue to be marginalised. In this context, the announcement of the funding arrangements for the new Children's Fund provides no indication that specific mechanisms will be created to ensure that black-led voluntary organisations will play a strong role in grant-giving; indeed, they appear implicitly to be excluded since the Treasury has indicated that the organisations holding and disbursing funds at a local level will be those 'with substantial experience of making grants'. That condition rules out most black and minority ethnic organisations.

Overall, while some of the PATs, such as PAT 3 (on enterprise and social exclusion), comment that their approach towards addressing black and minority ethnic issues 'has been to build our analysis and conclusions very much into the mainstream of our work',[19] the overall impression left by a detailed reading of all 18 PAT reports is that this continuing 'colour-blind' approach leaves many of the issues facing black and minority ethnic communities, and particularly the implicitly (and not infrequently explicitly) racist approaches of structures and organisations delivering services and making policies,[20] unaddressed.

RECENT DEVELOPMENTS

Two more recent outcomes from the work of the PATs provide, at best, mixed messages in relation to the issue of 'race' and ethnicity. The framework document, *National Strategy for Neighbourhood Renewal*, published by the SEU in April 2000 under a Foreword by the Prime Minister,[21] addresses the needs of ethnic minorities briefly in three ways: it notes again that they live disproportionately in deprived neighbourhoods, it observes that better data collection is needed to explore their needs, and it notes (yet again) the need to involve black and minority ethnic communities more fully both in the voluntary and community sector (for example, in regeneration programmes) and in individually-based initiatives, such as mentoring. However, there is again no analysis of the institutional barriers to achieving these ends or how they can be broken down. The other document, published in mid-2000,[22] draws together issues from all the PAT reports related to 'race' and ethnicity. Publication of this report may have been prompted by the heightened prominence of 'race' within political debate; the report at least provides formal recognition of an extensive agenda for further work, emphasising the responses to the SEU's earlier consultation (see below).

The future of the Social Exclusion Unit remains uncertain at the time of writing. A confidential internal review of the SEU conducted by the Cabinet Office in late 1999[23] indicated that the Unit's work should continue until 2002 (presumably with the longest feasible life of the present government in mind), but there has been no announcement as to whether the SEU would continue beyond the general election, should New Labour be returned to power. (As a flagship initiative of New Labour it would not be unlikely that a government of a different political persuasion would ditch it.) The review concluded that the SEU had largely been a success to date in raising the profile of social exclusion, that the Government had showed itself to be 'serious and genuine about involving the wider community in its thinking, knowledge-gathering and policy formulation...and had challenged vested interests where necessary'. It had faced severe difficulties, for example, needing more time to carry through implementation of its ideas and failing adequately to involve those working at the grassroots. None of this analysis particularly reflected on the SEU's failure effectively to address issues of 'race' and structural racism where its 'success' might be challenged more strongly.

WHAT NEXT FOR NEW LABOUR ON RACE?

The Government's response to the growth in the numbers of refugees and asylum seekers over the past four years shows at best, a schizophrenic attitude to issues of 'race' and ethnicity. This is demonstrated by the populist – and racist – stance of the Government towards immigration. On the one hand, it is prepared to consider extensive immigration of professional workers over the next few years to fill what it regards as significant gaps in the UK labour market. On the other hand, it has taken a punitive and at times quite vicious position towards refugees and asylum seekers arriving without any economic leverage. Those acquiring refugee status are predominantly incorporated into the body of those minorities among the poorest in

UK society. Asylum seekers resident in the UK are faced with an administrative system which is clearly failing to manage the demands placed upon it, a system which scapegoats asylum seekers rather than responding to their very real needs,[24] and which requires them to subsist on levels of support – in cash or kind (including the humiliating voucher system) – which are substantially below even inadequate income support levels. Research shows applications from asylum seekers of Asian, African-Caribbean and African origin have suffered disproportionate refusal levels.[25]

More encouragingly, however, an analysis of the responses to the consultation showed that, of the 39 topics identified for future SEU work programmes, one-third were explicitly concerned with 'race'; most of the remainder of course, such as children in care or economic inequality, should in any case have a strong 'race' dimension. Most interestingly, one topic identified was that of institutional racism, characterised as a 'Macpherson follow-up'. To date, however, no announcement has been made as to future work programmes for the SEU, presumably a result of uncertainty about the life of this Government. However, if the SEU were to continue, and were to address the issue of institutional racism in the context of social exclusion, the coming together of a number of initiatives, in particular the Lawrence Inquiry and its consequences, and the continuation of the SEU itself, would give some hope that in this deeply complex and contested area of 'race', the next administration might have the opportunity to demonstrate exactly what is meant by 'joined-up' government.

The death of Stephen Lawrence revealed the extent of racism within one major public agency and there seems little doubt from a wide range of other evidence that the same critique might be applied to the other major institutions which shape welfare and social policy. Given that many of these institutions continue, either inadvertently or not, to contribute to the immiseration of black and minority ethnic groups, the opportunity now presents itself for a future government to initiate a thorough-going analysis of public and private agencies responsible for delivering welfare and addressing poverty. The need for this is considerable, particularly as the otherwise wide-ranging *Report of the Commission on the Future of Multi-Ethnic Britain*,[26] failed adequately to address the deficiencies of much of social and welfare policy towards Britain's minorities. Were the next government to take up this challenge, a grounded assessment of the present government's term of office in the area of 'race' might then hopefully be 'too little, but not too late'.

NOTES

1 See for example, C Howarth et al, *Monitoring Poverty and Social Exclusion*, New Policy Institute, 1999; D Gordon et al, *Poverty and Social Exclusion in Britain*, Joseph Rowntree Foundation, 2000

2 G Craig, 'Race, Poverty and Social Security' in J Ditch (ed), *An Introduction to Social Security*, Routledge, 1999

3 M Howard, 'Ethnicity' in *Poverty: the facts* (revised edition), CPAG, forthcoming; see also T Modood, *Ethnic Minorities in Britain*, Policy Studies Institute, 1997

4 G Craig, 'Social Exclusion: introduction', *Research Matters*, 2000

5 See note 2

6 Sir W Macpherson, *The Stephen Lawrence Inquiry*, Cm 4262, The Stationery Office, 1999

7 Department of Social Security, *Opportunity for All: indicators of success*

8 Department of the Environment, Transport and the Regions 'Hilary Armstrong Launches Race Equality Guidance for New Deal for Communities Partnerships', Press Notice 1 March 2000

9 Department of the Environment, Transport and the Regions, *New Deal for Communities, Phase One Proposals, Guidance for Pathfinder Applicants*, 1998

10 Social Exclusion Unit, *Bringing Britain Together: a national strategy for neighbourhood renewal*, Cabinet Office, 1998

11 Social Exclusion Unit, *Truancy and School Exclusion*, 1998

12 Social Exclusion Unit, *Bridging the Gap: new opportunities for 16–18-year-olds not in education, employment or training*, 1999

13 See notes 2 and 3

14 Social Exclusion Unit, *Young People,* Report of PAT 12, 1999

15 Social Exclusion Unit, *Learning Lessons*, Report of PAT 16, 2000

16 Social Exclusion Unit, *Community Self-Help*, Report of PAT 9, 2000

17 Home Office, *Compact: getting it right together*, Cm 4100, 1998

18 G Craig and M Taylor, *Local Government and the Third Sector: papering over the cracks*, Compact Working Paper No. 3, University of Hull, 2000

19 Social Exclusion Unit, *Enterprise and Social Exclusion*, Report of PAT 13, 2000

20 B Parekh (Chair), *The Report of the Commission on the Future of Multi-Ethnic Britain*, Runnymede Trust, 2000

21 Social Exclusion Unit, *National Strategy for Neighbourhood Renewal: a framework for consultation*, Cabinet Office, 2000

22 Social Exclusion Unit, *Minority Ethnic Issues in Social Exclusion and Neighbourhood Renewal: a guide to the work of the Social Exclusion Unit and the Policy Action Teams so far*, Cabinet Office, 2000

23 Cabinet Office, *Confidential Review of the Social Exclusion Unit*, 1999

24 See note 20

25 *A Right to Family Life*, National Association of Citizens Advice Bureaux, 1996

26 See note 20

Conclusion
Geoff Fimister

Our authors have analysed the Government's performance in a number of policy areas relating to different aspects of poverty. In line with CPAG's approach, as set out in the Introduction, we asked them to be scrupulously balanced in giving credit where credit is due, while levying criticism where it is deserved. The broad drift of what our contributors have had to say is that the scale of the problem is immense; the Government's recognition that there is a problem which needs to be addressed is a big step forward; and that the efforts made so far are mostly (although not entirely) welcome as far as they go, but that much more needs to be done.

It should also be borne in mind that this book has been compiled during a period when, apart from a short period after the fuel price protests of September 2000, the Government has enjoyed a substantial lead in the opinion polls. Nevertheless, it cannot be assumed that the next government will inevitably be a Labour regime with a working majority – other scenarios may come to pass. Cross-party commitment to a target date for the abolition of child poverty would therefore have been very welcome. CPAG has called for such a commitment on a number of occasions. Realistically, though, there is still not a consensus – and political parties still tend, on most issues, to shy away from conferring credibility on their opponents' policies by signing up to them too readily. Our best bet for ensuring the continuation of an anti-poverty perspective in government, not only across general elections but also beyond economic fluctuations, is to try to raise the profile of the issue to such a degree that governments will not be able to get away with neglecting it. A recognition of the indecency of poverty must become part of our common culture.

What, then, have been our contributors' main preoccupations, where they have said 'must do better'?

PRIORITIES FOR THE NEXT PARLIAMENT

Jonathan Bradshaw illustrates that, after a very poor start, the government has made substantial progress in tackling child poverty. As Bradshaw points out, there are qualifications to be made to this. Firstly, the figures suggest that some of the poorest children have still lost out. Secondly, the POLIMOD figures that he uses show the position before housing costs have been taken into account. CPAG regards 'after-housing costs' as more realistic in establishing actual disposable incomes – and the numbers in poverty on the latter measure tend to be significantly higher. Nevertheless, as Bradshaw says, 'there is no doubt that when the election takes place there will have been a substantial reduction in poverty, particularly child poverty, by any measure you care to use.'

Significantly, he also shows that a great deal more could have been done had the Chancellor not decided to forego £2.44 billion by reducing the standard rate of income tax. This tax cut was a manifestation of the Government's political balancing act in trying to keep a broad cross-section of the public on board. This is an understandable ambition, but the public should not be underestimated – if the case is put clearly, most people can understand why we all have an interest in trying to keep the next generation out of poverty. Bradshaw also points out that the task is going to get harder as the Government starts to focus on those more deeply submerged. He argues convincingly that the question of vertical redistribution – 'taxing and spending' – cannot be ducked. It follows that a government which is serious about poverty will have to engage the public in the arguments – and win them.

Turning specifically to children's benefits and credits, Martin Barnes and I have set out a number of specific issues which need to be addressed in planning for the proposed integrated child credit. A major overall issue, though, is the need to protect and develop the role of child benefit; the integrated child credit must not become a vehicle to undermine it. Setting the right levels for child benefit and the integrated child credit is also crucial, reflecting Bradshaw's point concerning the scale of the remaining task in digging children out of poverty. We also stress the need to get the administration right, including allowing sufficient time for software design and testing. Administrative failure is a real threat where different agencies are required to run a combined operation.

In the field of employment policy, Richard Exell welcomes the integrated approach to employment services which is a key aspiration of the Government's approach, while calling for more emphasis to be given to the needs of particularly disadvantaged groups such as disabled or older workers. He warns, though, of the continuing trend towards greater compulsion, becoming more severe for those traditionally affected while expanding to cover further groups of claimants. This approach could distort and undermine the good intentions of the overall programme. He also calls for action to achieve a more adequate minimum wage, arguing that £4.50 or £5.00 an hour would be perfectly feasible.

George Smith and Teresa Smith, addressing the interaction between education and poverty, welcome the Government's commitment to tackling the problem, but consider the jury still to be out as regards progress so far. They see the legacy of the tight financial regime which followed the 1997 election as a limitation yet to be fully overcome, as is the continuation of 'a large part of the policies of previous government'. A cleaner break with the latter and a continuing willingness to prioritise the needs of 'disadvantaged areas, schools and pupils' must be looked for in any second term. They further argue that the 'necessary intermediate institutions between central government and schools' and the role of local education authorities need to be resolved; while there remains also the task of 'consolidating and systematising the rash of initiatives aiming to tackle educational disadvantage'.

As regards policy on health, Mary Shaw and her colleagues locate future progress in health standards among disadvantaged families firmly in the context of continuing efforts to attack financial poverty – they are in no doubt as to the critical relationship between the two. They also draw attention to the health implications of inequality in access to and outcomes of education, echoing the themes of the previous chapter. They argue that the financial disadvantage faced by disabled children and their families and by lone parent families needs pressingly to be addressed. Finally, they call for specific attention to the health needs of young people who are looked after by local authorities or who are homeless, calling among other things, for the restoration of benefit entitlements to 16 and 17-year-olds.

Matthew Waters also identifies homelessness as a key issue, requiring both immediate action and determined measures in the next parliament. He further points out that licensing of poor quality accommodation in the private rented sector is a manifesto commitment from the last general election which is still outstanding. He also points to the need for greater investment in social housing and for a reform of housing benefit which will address both the plight of tenants faced with shortfalls in meeting the rent and the administrative problems which beset the scheme.

In his discussion of neighbourhood renewal, Pete Alcock stresses the importance of local targets as part of any national strategy – making clear that national and local action are interdependent. 'Social inclusion can be promoted by local action…but this must be placed within the wider context of social exclusion and social polarisation'. He also calls for local action which challenges paternalism and stigmatisation of the neighbourhoods concerned and which actively strives to enable local people to participate. Evaluation of initiatives must be concerned with processes as much as with outcomes.

Gary Craig is scathing in his assessment of the treatment of refugees and asylum seekers. Clearly, there is a pressing need for the next government to address this. As Craig points out, it is not good enough to extend a civilised welcome only to those who are expected to fill skill shortages which are inconveniencing the rest of us. However, the need to tackle racism along with poverty and social exclusion goes much deeper than this. Citing the lessons regarding institutional racism to be drawn from the Stephen Lawrence Inquiry, Craig calls on the next government to establish 'a thorough-going analysis of public and private agencies responsible for delivering welfare and addressing poverty'.

There are also questions of language, style and emphasis which the next administration could usefully bear in mind. I commented in the Introduction that there is a tendency to 'balance' progressive social measures with a populist rhetoric which often stigmatises benefit claimants. Other contributions have made similar points. We can do without this; the drive against poverty in the twenty-first century needs to leave behind the divisive language of the deserving versus the undeserving poor.

We would certainly not claim that the above agenda is comprehensive, but it does represent a summary of a number of the key issues which the next government needs to address if the abolition of child poverty is to remain a central policy objective.

I commented earlier in these concluding remarks that a recognition of the indecency of poverty needs to become part of our common culture. The debate surrounding the forthcoming general election provides us all with an opportunity to push this perspective further towards the centre of political discourse. We hope that this book may be able to make some contribution to that purpose. Is there 'an end in sight' for child poverty? Our society has the resources; we need only to maintain and strengthen the political will.

APPENDIX I

NEW LABOUR DIARY

1997
MAY
Labour wins the general election. Harriet Harman is appointed
Secretary of State for Social Security; Frank Field is Minister for
Welfare Reform. In the Queen's Speech, Tony Blair announces a range
of measures including 'welfare to work' and a national minimum wage.
The Government continues with plans to introduce tougher
conditions for benefit claims and to re-vamp the Appeals Service.

JUNE
The New Deal for young people is announced. Sir Donald Acheson is
commissioned to produce an updated version of the Black Report on
inequalities in health. William Hague is elected leader of the
Conservative Party.

JULY
The Chancellor of the Exchequer, Gordon Brown, delivers the first
Labour Budget for 18 years. Included are measures to promote
employability, moving people from welfare to work. The New Deal,
which will be financed by a one-off windfall tax on excess profits from
privatised utilities, is launched in eight pilot areas. Tessa Jowell
announces a new strategy to improve public health. The Education
Minister announces plans to abolish maintenance grants for higher
education and to introduce a means-tested annual tuition fee of
£1,000.

AUGUST
Plans to set up a Social Exclusion Unit are announced. The number of
people out of work has fallen to 1,550,000 – the lowest level since
September 1980. Harriet Harman decides to press ahead with plans to
scrap extra benefits for lone parents.

SEPTEMBER
Gordon Brown restores the Labour Party's commitment to full
employment.

OCTOBER

Shelter warns that youth homelessness will rise as a result of recent benefit cuts. The Child Support Agency announces a major shake-up. Latest figures from *Households Below Average Income* show that the poorest 30 per cent are relatively worse off than in 1979.

NOVEMBER

In his pre-Budget report, Gordon Brown announces plans for a new tax credit system. The National Minimum Wage Bill is published. A letter to the Chancellor is signed by 120 MPs, condemning the cuts to lone parents' benefits. Research from the Institute of Child Health shows that social class has a powerful influence on health.

DECEMBER

A Royal Commission on the long-term care of older people is announced. The Social Exclusion Unit is launched.

1998
JANUARY

The New Deal for young people aged 18-24 is launched in 12 pilot areas. The Government announces 20,000 additional childcare places as part of its £300 million childcare strategy. *Social Trends 1998* ranks Britain ninth out of eleven EU countries on expenditure on social protection benefits.

FEBRUARY

The Government's public health strategy, *Our Healthier Nation*, is launched.

MARCH

Gordon Brown introduces his second Budget. Children's benefits are to be increased ahead of inflation for families both in and out of work. Tax and benefit reforms will be delivered through a working families' tax credit, which will replace family credit from October 1999. Frank Field unveils the Government's Green Paper on welfare reform, *New Ambitions for Our Country: a new contract for welfare*. The Government pledges that every child will have a nursery, school or playgroup place by September.

APRIL

Gordon Brown launches the £3.5 billion 'welfare to work' programme.

JUNE

The Government launches a Disability Benefits Forum to examine benefits for long-term sick and disabled people. A two-tier minimum wage is announced.

JULY

The Social Exclusion Unit's report, *Tackling Rough Sleepers*, estimates that there are 2,000 people sleeping on the streets each night in England. Tony Blair appoints a homelessness czar to tackle the problem. The Comprehensive Spending Review announces an extra £40 billion over three years for education and health. Most of the money, however, will not be paid until the second and third years of the review. A new education maintenance allowance is announced. Frank Field resigns and Harriet Harman is sacked in the ministerial reshuffle. Alistair Darling takes over as Secretary of State for Social Security.

AUGUST

The Government launches seven health action zones with £15 million of extra funding. It is reported that Alistair Darling has been ordered to cut the £7.6 billion incapacity benefit bill by 25 per cent.

SEPTEMBER

The Transport Bill is dropped from the Queen's Speech. The National Consultation on the Rights of the Disabled is launched. The Social Exclusion Unit publishes another report, *Bringing Britain Together: a national strategy for neighbourhood renewal*; the Government responds by announcing the £800 million New Deal for communities. Britain has the highest proportion of lone-parent families in Europe, according to Eurostat.

OCTOBER

The New Deal for lone parents goes national.

NOVEMBER

The Queen's Speech sets out the reform of disability benefits: the creation of a Disability Rights Commission; the development of stakeholder pensions; and a 'single gateway' for all benefits and tax credits. The Green Paper *Supporting the Family* is launched – tackling child poverty is one of the five areas targeted. The Acheson report, *Inequalities in Health*, is published. The Office for National Statistics publishes new definitions of social class.

DECEMBER

The Family Budget Unit's report, *Low Cost but Acceptable*, highlights the discrepancy between benefit rates and living costs.

1999
JANUARY

A new strand of the Government's 'welfare to work' policy is announced, targeting 50–64-year-olds. A report by the National Audit Office shows that the Government has £2 billion from unpaid benefits.

FEBRUARY

The Immigration and Asylum Bill is published, proposing to replace asylum seekers' right to welfare benefits with a system of subsistence vouchers. The Welfare Reform and Pensions Bill is also published, which includes the new Single Gateway and proposed changes to incapacity benefit. The Government announces that it intends to publish an annual poverty audit.

MARCH

In the Beveridge lecture, Tony Blair pledges to end child poverty in 20 years. The Budget includes further increases in the real value of children's benefits.

APRIL

The national minimum wage becomes law. A Friends of the Earth report highlights the relationship between the poorest areas and levels of pollution.

MAY

A new education maintenance allowance, piloted in selected areas of the country, offers children of poorer parents up to £40 a week to stay in education. New measures to tackle fuel poverty include grants of up to £1,800 to install central heating. Leading disability groups quit the Disability Benefits Forum in protest over proposed cuts to incapacity benefit. Sixty-five Labour MPs vote against the proposed changes.

JUNE

The Social Exclusion Unit publishes its long-awaited teenage pregnancy report. The Government announces £60 million to combat the problem.

JULY

The child support White Paper, *Children's Rights and Parents' Responsibilities*, is published. A British Medical Association report, *Growing Up in Britain*, highlights the degree of inequality in children's health. *Our Healthier Nation*, the White Paper on public health, is published. Sure Start, the intervention for 0–3-year-olds, is launched.

SEPTEMBER

The official poverty audit, *Opportunity for All*, is published and lists 32 poverty indicators. Ten million pensioners will receive £100 each towards their Winter fuel bills as part of the bid to end fuel poverty.

OCTOBER

'Quality Protects', the £375 million programme to support children in care, is launched. State pensions will rise by only 75p next year because of the low rate of inflation. Working families' tax credit and disabled person's tax credit are launched

NOVEMBER

The Queen's Speech includes a Child Support and Pensions Bill. Children in poor families are over three times more likely to have mental health problems, according to the Office for National Statistics.

DECEMBER

The health gap between rich and poor has never been wider, according to research published by Bristol University.

2000
JANUARY

Eighty Labour backbenchers sign a motion condemning the proposed 75p pensions rise.

MARCH

The Chancellor announces a package of measures designed to lift a further 400,000 children out of poverty. The Budget again provides for improved means-tested benefits and tax credits for children, but this time a small increase in child benefit from April 2001, which will in effect do no more than preserve its value.

JUNE

The Government admits that the New Deal programme is much more expensive than anticipated. The cost of placing an individual in work is £11,000 per job – much higher than the £4,000 originally estimated.

JULY

According to *Households Below Average Income*, the number of households on less than half average income rose by 300,000 in Labour's first year in office. The Comprehensive Spending Review includes a new Children's Fund, worth £450 million over three years; plans to make the New Deal for young unemployed permanent; more than £3 billion for neighbourhood renewal strategies; and the expansion of Sure Start.

SEPTEMBER

Eighteen per cent of children in Britain are deprived of two or more everyday necessities, according to the *Poverty and Social Exclusion Report 2000* carried out jointly by several leading universities and the Office for National Statistics.

OCTOBER

The Human Rights Act comes into force. The Government pledges an extra 600,000 childcare places as part of its strategy to get lone parents into employment. The second edition of the Government's poverty report, *Opportunity for All, One Year On: making a difference*, is published.

NOVEMBER

Measures announced in the pre-Budget report include a £5 increase in pensions for single people and £8 for couples, and an increase in the proposed children's tax credit from £8.50 to £10.00 a week. The Free Fruit for Schools pilot is launched.

DECEMBER

The third New Policy Institute poverty survey is published. Of the 49 indicators compared year on year, 17 have improved, 23 are the same and 9 have worsened.

CPAG's Policy publications package –
high quality information, excellent value

Join CPAG as a Policy member to receive our hard-hitting Poverty Publications three times a year.

They bring you unique insights into poverty in the UK, research and statistics, and policy proposals for eradicating poverty. As a member you will receive them immediately they are published, post free. In addition you will receive:

- **Poverty** magazine three times a year, with informative and stimulating articles on current poverty issues (normal price £3.95 per issue)
- **Campaigns newsletter** six times a year – updates you on what CPAG is doing
- Exclusive member discounts on CPAG handbooks and courses.

Policy membership costs just £30 a year.

For a leaflet about other types of CPAG membership including publications packages please contact us at the address below.

To: CPAG, 94 White Lion Street, London N1 9PF

Please enrol me/my organisation as a Policy member* for one year at £30.

* Please do not use this form to renew if you are already a member – you will receive a renewal form automatically.

☐ I enclose a cheque for £_____ payable to CPAG

☐ I would like to pay £_____ by Visa/Access/Delta/Switch (please delete as appropriate)

Card No: _____

Issue No (Switch) _____ Expiry date: _____

Cardholder Signature:_____

Name_____

Company/Organisation (if joining on its behalf) _____

Address_____

_____

_____ Postcode _____

Tel _____ Fax _____ E-mail _____

When Children Pay
US welfare reform and its implications for UK policy
Rosemary J Link and Anthony A Bibus, with Karen Lyons
Foreword by David Bull

The concepts behind 'welfare to work' – the 'New Deal' – are imported from the United States. But how relevant is the American experience of welfare reform to the UK, and what lessons are there for a British Government aiming to abolish child poverty within twenty years?

When Children Pay aims to reach a critical understanding of both US and UK approaches to poverty and income maintenance, highlighting what may work and what is unlikely to work when transplanted from the US to the UK. As well as analysing the US approach, it presents evidence of its success or otherwise in alleviating child poverty. The authors conclude with recommendations for British policy makers to take on board when planning to abolish child poverty.

ISBN 1 901698 15 7 Published 2000 £9.95

Poverty First Hand
Poor people speak for themselves
Peter Beresford, David Green, Ruth Lister and Kirsty Woodard

Poverty First Hand is a unique account of poor people's own analysis of poverty; its definition, causes and effects; their views on government and media treatment of poverty; their views on what policies are needed and what part poor people should play in them. It is based on a two-year participatory project, meeting nationwide with a wide range of groups of people with direct experience of poverty.

Poverty First Hand offers a forceful, first-hand analysis of poverty in the UK which has profound implications both for poverty debates and the future of anti-poverty policy.

ISBN 0 946744 89 0 Published 1999 £9.95

To order, please send payment to
CPAG, 94 White Lion Street, London N1 9PF.
Please add £2.95 p&p if your order totals over £10.